Student's Review Manual for John A. Garraty

The American Nation

A History of the United States to 1877

THIRD EDITION

Ellen Howell Myers

San Antonio College

Harper & Row, Publishers

New York, Evanston, San Francisco, London

Student's Review Manual for Garraty THE AMERICAN NATION
A History of the United States to 1877, Third Edition

Standard Book Number: 06-042264-5

Introduction

The purpose of this Student's Review Manual is to help you study and review the textbook THE AMERICAN NATION (Third Edition) by John Garraty. The Manual is not a replacement for or a condensed version of the text, but instead a guide to its major points. The textbook is like a tree: the trunk contains important themes and generalizations, holding together and giving life to the branches of ideas, events, and personalities which have made history. The Student's Review Manual points out the major branches. These facts are useless unless they are attached to a major theme in a meaningful way.

Each chapter of the Review Manual is organized in the same manner. First there is a CHAPTER CHECKLIST, which summarizes the major points covered. This checklist is followed by a list of OTHER TERMS TO IDENTIFY, which provides further information to help you understand the material. The items are listed in the order that they appear in the chapter. After OTHER TERMS is a GLOSSARY with definitions of words and terms that may not be familiar to you, listed alphabetically. Then there is a list of other words you should be able to define, and a selection of SAMPLE QUESTIONS: multiple choice, true-false, and some matching.

HOW TO USE THE MANUAL FOR BEST RESULTS

First, read the assigned chapter in the textbook, keeping the Manual close at hand in order to look up unfamiliar terms or phrases in the GLOSSARY. It is a good idea, too, to keep a dictionary nearby in case you need to be sure of the meaning of certain words, particularly those listed under DEFINE THE FOLLOWING.

To review the chapter, read the CHAPTER CHECKLIST. You will find, along with the major points, other features such as small charts and PRESIDENTS' BOXES, the latter outlining important dates and events in the life of each President. OTHER TERMS TO IDENTIFY will help remind you of additional facts covered in the text.

After studying the textbook and the Student's Review Manual, spot check your memory of the material by answering the SAMPLE QUESTIONS. They will also give you practice in answering objective questions on quizzes and exams. If you find you cannot answer one or more of the questions, go back to the text and to the Review Manual for further study.

Ellen Howell Myers
San Antonio College

Contents

Portfolio 1
The Heritage of Africa

CHARACTERISTICS

A wide variety of cultures flourished along the west coast of Africa in the 15th through the 18th centuries. But many Africans of the area shared common characteristics.

Bondage. Strong clans overran weaker ones and established a semifeudal relationship in which the conquered peoples became vassals and paid tribute to the victor. Sometimes the defeated society would be enslaved, and either kept by their captors or sold.

Religion. Most Africans believed in a creator god who could be influenced to provide the necessities of life through the intercession of lesser gods. All things, whether living or inanimate, were considered to be embued with spirits.

Ancestor cults. Africans did not believe that death destroyed the vital forces within and therefore ancestors remained influential in the affairs of the living.

Art. Sculpture in wood, metal, or stone often had religious or political significance, although it could serve other purposes, such as the gold weights of the Ashanti on pp. P1-VIII-IX.

Initiation into adulthood. Many Africans had special rites to mark the "coming of age" of young people ready to accept their responsibilities. Art objects used in these ceremonies can be seen on pp. P1-III, XXI.

Secret societies. Associations of men or of women, chiefly among the clans along the Windward Coast. The men's secret societies were the important force in these communities and derived their authority from ancestor spirits.

GEOGRAPHICAL AND POLITICAL AREAS

Note the following areas on the map in this Manual.

Senegambia. The area between the Senegal and Gambia rivers in which a number of tribes lived. It was the first region south of the Sahara desert to experience contact with Europeans. By 1500 they exchanged gold, ivory, pepper, gum arabic, and some slaves for horses, fabric, and metalware. By by the mid 1600's, slaves had become their most important export.

The Windward Coast. An area along the Atlantic coast, within the "hump" of Africa. In this region life was regulated by men's secret societies, and the ancestor cult stressed the continuance and order of the clan.

The Gold Coast. The Ashanti people moved to present-day Ghana in the 1600's and by 1700 had established a confederation of tribes. The area flourished because of gold resources and a strong military. At first Europeans were attracted to the area by gold, but later a slave trade developed. The Ashanti generally did not sell directly to Europeans, but used the coastal Fanti people as middlemen.

Dahomey. In the 1600's the Fon people moved to the Abomey plateau and founded a monarchy which stressed the individual's responsibility to the king rather than the usual pattern of the king acting as a father figure. Dahomey was a military state and sold its war captives as slaves in exchange for guns.

Oyo. A nation made up of over 20 separate states and dominated by the Yoruba, who proved a stable monarchy. The people lived in towns, where trade and crafts flourished. Oyo reached its zenith in the 1700's, and was famous for its cavalry. But conflict broke out between the military and the trading interests, and the latter won, concentrating on the slave trade, which led to Oyo's collapse.

Benin. A nation which particularly flourished in the 1400's and 1500's and which was devoted to ancestor worship. Craft guilds were an important element, and brass, obtained through trade, was a favorite medium of sculptors. After the Portuguese arrived in 1485 the oba, or king of Benin, tried to limit trade with Europeans, but some of its provinces began to sell slaves for firearms and the nation declined in power.

Bonny and Old Calabar. Coastal city-states in the delta of the Niger River. In this area there were small political groups rather than large kingdoms but they were interrelated economically by the river trade and had similar institutions. These river ports became centers of the slave trade.

Kongo. A well-established state when the first Portuguese mission arrived in 1485. The ruler welcomed Christian missionaries, diplomats, and merchants, but by the 1520's slave trade was flourishing and the Kongo kingdom was on the decline. It was overrun by the warlike Yaka in 1568.

SLAVE TRADE

The traffic in Negro slaves was not a European innovation. Both native rulers and Arab traders had engaged in it for years, but with the arrival of the Portuguese in 1443 it reached enormous proportions. Craving European products such as liquor and firearms, African chiefs sold fellow Africans, sometimes their own subjects, to the Portuguese, Dutch, French, and English merchants.

"Trust trade." The practice in the major African ports of European traders entrusting goods to local merchants which they in turn carried to the interior and exchanged for slaves. The slaves were brought back to the coast in coffles, that is, long lines of slaves chained together.

Middle Passage. The transporting of slaves from Africa to islands in the Caribbean Sea, a journey lasting two or three months. Conditions on the ships were crowded and inhuman, and approximately 20 to 30 per cent died on the Middle Passage.

"Seasoning." A term referring to the process by which African slaves were forced to adapt to new conditions and a new environment, that is, acclimatized. Slaves were sometimes "seasoned" in the West Indian islands before being sent to North or South America to be sold.

GLOSSARY

cowry shell. The shell of any of a variety of marine mollusks, which is glossy and often brightly marked. Cowry shells were a form of currency used in many parts of Africa.

gum arabic. A substance exuded by specific African trees of the mimosa family, which was used in the manufacture of candies, glue, and in general as a thickener. Gum arabic was one of the items which the Africans traded to the Europeans.

pantheon. All the gods of a people. Most of the African people worshipped a creator god and a pantheon of lesser dieties. The term is derived from the circular temple in Rome, completed in 27 B.C., which was dedicated to all the gods.

pectoral mask. A mask or image which is worn on the chest. An ivory pectoral mask, probably worn by the oba of Benin, is pictured on p. Pl-XVII.

secular. Pertaining to life in the world, rather than something spiritual or religious. Much of the art of the Africans served religious purposes, and secular objects of art, such as the salt-cellar on p. Pl-I, were rare.

terra-cotta. In Italian the term literally means "cooked earth." It is a hard, semifired, waterproof ceramic clay used in pottery and building. An Ibo altar made of terra-cotta is shown on p. Pl-XVIII.

DEFINE THE FOLLOWING, USING THE DICTIONARY IF NECESSARY

analogous
cassava
enervated
estuary
foibles
indigenous
insidious
licentiousness
nomadic
pestilential

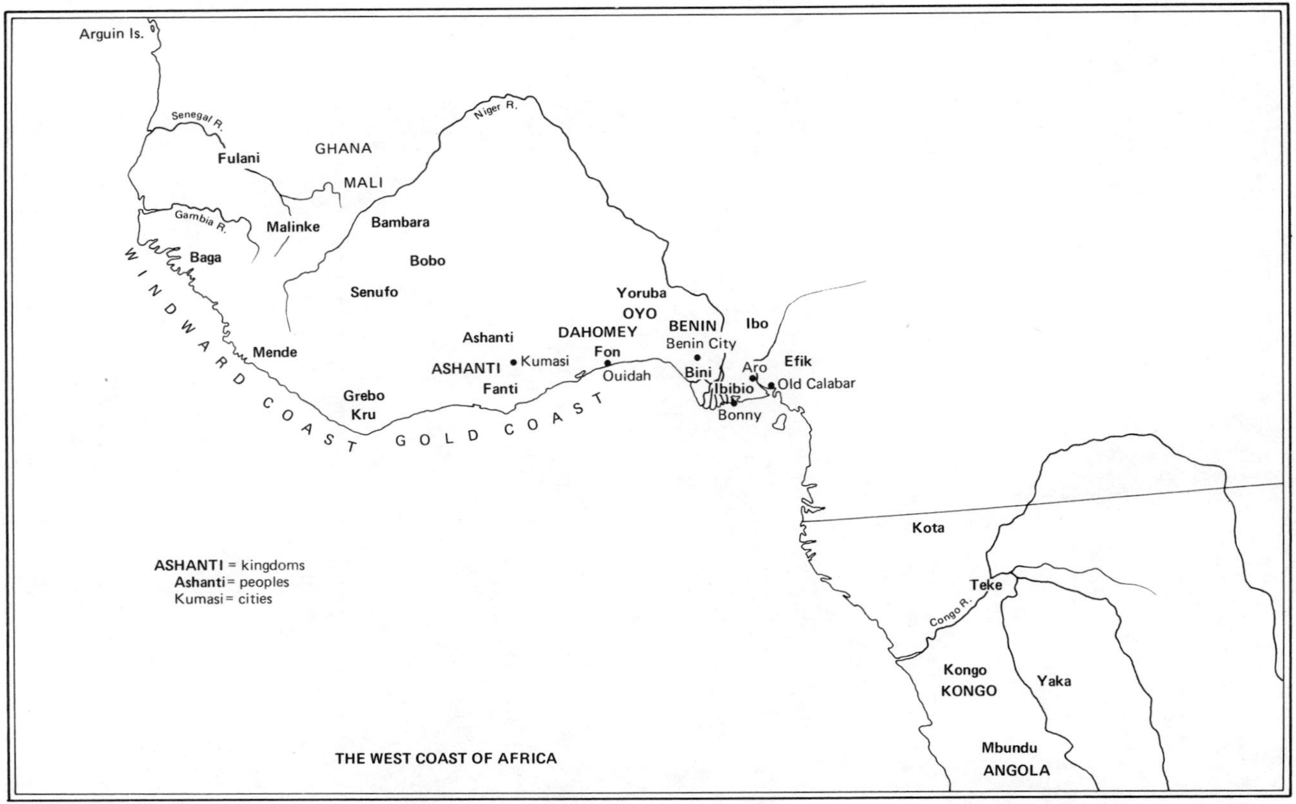

THE WEST COAST OF AFRICA

1

The Age of Discovery and Settlement

CHAPTER CHECKLIST

SPANISH BEGINNINGS IN AMERICA

Christopher Columbus (1451-1506). The modern "discoverer" of America who, sailing under the Spanish flag, made four voyages to the western hemisphere from 1492 to 1504, and died still believing that he had reached Asia. See the picture of Columbus, p. 8.

Amerigo Vespucci (1454-1512). The Italian after whom America was named. His written account of voyages in 1499 and 1501 along the South American coast caused Martin Waldseemüller, a German mapmaker, to be convinced that Vespucci was the discoverer and thus the land should be named for him.

ENGLISH BEGINNINGS

Sir Humphrey Gilbert (1537?-1583). An Englishman who made two attempts (1578, 1583) to establish colonies in America. After the second attempt, in Newfoundland, Gilbert and the colonists decided to return home to England and their ship sank in a storm off the Azores Islands.

Sir Walter Raleigh (1552?-1618). Half-brother of Gilbert who made several unsuccessful attempts (1585, 1587) to settle colonists on Roanoke Island, off the coast of North Carolina. Raleigh named the east coast of North America "Virginia" in honor of his unmarried queen, Elizabeth I. Note the picture of Raleigh on p. 14.

Richard Hakluyt (1552?-1616). An English authority on the Americas in the late 16th century who stressed the need of the English crown to promote and financially support colonization in America. He stated the advantages in an essay, Discourse on Western Planting.

VIRGINIA

1606, London Company. A joint-stock company composed of London merchants with royal permission to colonize what was then called southern Virginia.

1607, Jamestown. Colony founded by the London Company which became the first permanent English settlement in the New World.

John Rolfe (1585-1622). His introduction of a milder strain of tobacco into Virginia provided a marketable cash crop and eventually made the colony economically successful. Rolfe also helped the colony by his marriage to Pocahontas, daughter of the Powhatan chief.

1619, House of Burgesses. A governmental body of delegates chosen in each district who met at Jamestown to advise the governor on local matters. It is considered the beginning of representative government in America.

RELIGIOUS DIVISION IN ENGLAND

Anglicans. Members of the official Church of England, which had been founded when Henry VIII broke with the Roman Catholic Church in the 1530's.

Puritans. Members of the Church of England who wanted to "purify" it by discarding Roman Catholic practices which still remained.

Separatists. Members of the Church of England who thought it too corrupt, and therefore separated from it.

MASSACHUSETTS

1620, Plymouth Plantation founded. About one-third of the colonists were Pilgrims, an English separatist group which had moved to Holland before sailing for the New World.

1620, Mayflower Compact. A document signed on board the ship, the *Mayflower*, in which the passengers agreed to make laws and to abide by them.

November, 1621: Thanksgiving feast. The Plymouth settlers celebrated a bountiful harvest with their Indian neighbors, thus establishing an American tradition.

1630, Massachusetts Bay Company. Composed of English Puritans, settled about 1,000 colonists in the Boston area.

John Winthrop. First governor of the Massachusetts Bay

colony.

freemen. Adult male settlers of the Massachusetts Bay colony who were permitted to participate in political affairs. Originally about one hundred men were selected by the leaders of the colony and thereafter only Puritan church members were included and allowed to vote.

General Court. The name used to refer to the colonial legislature of Massachusetts.

CONNECTICUT

1636. Reverend Thomas Hooker and his Puritan congregation moved from Massachusetts and founded Hartford.

1639, Fundamental Orders. A governmental charter set up for the Connecticut River valley towns. It was patterned after the Massachusetts system, although male non-church members could vote.

RHODE ISLAND

1636, Roger Williams. He left Salem, Massachusetts, and founded Providence, Rhode Island, on land purchased from the Indians. His colony was the first to separate church and state.

Anne Hutchinson. A Boston resident who, like Williams, disagreed with the official Puritan theology and led some of her followers to settle in Rhode Island.

MARYLAND

1634. First settlers arrived in Maryland, a proprietary colony founded by Cecilius Calvert, whose title was Lord Baltimore.

1649, Toleration Act. A grant of freedom of religion to anyone who professed to believe in Jesus Christ. Lord Baltimore, a Catholic, had hoped that Maryland would be exclusively a Roman Catholic colony, when members of his own faith were quickly outnumbered by Protestants, he tried to protect them with this act.

CAROLINA

1670. First settlers arrived in Carolina, a proprietary colony named in honor of King Charles I of England.

Fundamental Constitution. A plan of government which tried, unsuccessfully, to promote a feudal society in Carolina with landholding "landgraves" and caciques" and peasants called "leet-men."

1712. The colony separated into North and South Carolina.

NEW YORK

1624. Dutch West India Company founded a colony known as New Netherland.

1664. England captured the colony. It was granted to the king's brother, James, Duke of York, who in 1685 became King James II.

NEW JERSEY

1664. This proprietary colony attracted settlers by offering land on easy terms, freedom of religion, and a democratic system of local government. By the 1680's all the proprietors were Quakers, and members of that religious group settled here in large numbers.

PENNSYLVANIA

1681. A proprietary grant was given to William Penn, a Quaker, who considered his colony a "Holy Experiment."

Quakers, or Society of Friends. A Christian religious group started in England by George Fox, who admonished his followers to "tremble at the name of the Lord," thus the name Quakers. They required no rituals or ministers and their place of worship was called a meeting house, where the men sat on one side and the women on the other. They spoke one by one as the Inner Light, the illumination from God within each soul, spoke to them.

GEORGIA

1732. James Oglethorpe founded Savannah. This proprietary colony was founded originally as a new chance for men in English debtors' prisons and also as a buffer against the Spanish in Florida.

OTHER TERMS TO IDENTIFY

Prince Henry the Navigator. A 15th century Portuguese prince who from his court at Sagres encouraged the advance of navigational knowledge and the development of Portugal's trade with Atlantic islands and the African coast. See his picture on p. 7.

1494, Treaty of Tordesillas. A treaty signed at Tordesillas, Spain, by Spain and Portugal which moved the 1493 Papal

Line of Demarcation to 370 leagues (1 league= 3 miles) west of the Cape Verde Islands. All non-Christian lands to the west of the line were reserved for Spanish commerce and colonization, those to the east of it were for Portugal. This treaty supposedly gave the New World, except for what became Brazil, to Spain, a claim which other European nations soon chose to ignore.

Requerimiento. A document which Spanish conquerors read to American natives before attacking them. If the Indians did not recognize the authority of the Pope and the Spanish monarch, whose importance was duly explained in the Requirement, then the conquerors could consider the attack a "just war" and proceed.

Black Legend. A term used to criticize the Spaniards' allegedly cruel treatment of the Indians. The propaganda was initiated by the Spanish friar, Las Casas, who was called "Protector of the Indians," and then was fanned by Spain's Protestant enemies, especially England and the Netherlands.

Captain John Smith. An English soldier of fortune who spent two years in the early Jamestown colony. He encouraged the colonists to raise food and trade with the Indians rather than search for gold. He also explored, mapped, and named the New England area.

proprietor. A man who was granted a large amount of land by the king; he in turn gave or sold his land to settlers, retaining political power over them. Eight of the thirteen original English colonies started as proprietary colonies.

joint-stock company. A company formed by merchant capitalists who shared the expenses, and the losses, of a colonizing or trading expedition. The London Company, which founded Jamestown, is an example.

GLOSSARY

Antinomianism. A form of Christian belief that says faith alone is necessary to salvation. Anne Hutchinson, a Massachusetts Puritan, was persecuted for preaching her own variety of Antinomianism.

commonwealth. The official title of some U.S. states, including Virginia, Maryland, Massachusetts, and Pennsylvania. For example, officially one says the Commonwealth of Massachusetts, rather than the state of Massachusetts. The term is used to mean a nation or state governed by the people.

Crusades. Christian military expeditions from 1095 to about 1290 to recover the Holy Land, present day Israel, from the Moslems. These travels furthered European interest in oriental products. Note the map entitled "Trade and Trade Routes in the 14th Century" on p. 4.

dissenter. One who refuses to accept the doctrines of the established or national church. For example, the Quakers were dissenters from the Church of England.

Indies. A vague term used on early maps to describe Asia and nearby islands. Columbus thought he had reached the Indies, and thus called the natives Indians.

Inquisition. A special Roman Catholic Church proceeding designed to discover and suppress heresy; in Spain, it was controlled by the monarchs who introduced the Inquisition in the colonies in 1569.

Marco Polo (1254?-1324?). A Venetian who journeyed overland to China and wrote an account of his adventures in the service of Kublai Khan. This book became the chief Western source of information about the East.

New England. The northeastern region of present day United States was christened "New England" by Captain John Smith after an expedition to the area of Maine in 1614. Today the New England states include Maine, New Hampshire, Vermont, Massachusetts, Rhode Island, and Connecticut.

patroon. An individual receiving a large land grant from the Dutch government. He had to settle at least fifty people on this grant, after which it became an hereditary fief. Patroons were granted land in New Netherland, present day New York.

Pennsylvania "Dutch." German (Deutsch) settlers in Pennsylvania, attracted by William Penn's glowing descriptions of his colony.

primogeniture. The right of the eldest son to inherit all of his father's estate, particularly if he died intestate, that is, having made no legal will. This medieval tradition prevailed in the South, the middle colonies with the exception of Pennsylvania, and Rhode Island.

Privy Council. A group of fifteen to twenty of the British monarch's principal ministers who helped him watch over the entire administration of the kingdom. After the 17th century the Council declined in importance, and today it is simply an honorary group.

Protestant. In the 16th century, one who protested the practices of the Roman Catholic Church. Today the term refers to a non-Roman Catholic Christian, such as a Lutheran, an Anglican, or a Presbyterian.

Protestant Reformation. The effort in the 16th century to reconstitute the teachings of Christianity in western Europe, which resulted in the creation of Protestant churches separate from the Roman Catholic Church.

Salic law. An old Germanic law prohibiting a woman from succeeding to the throne as the ruling monarch of a country.

West Indies. The chain of islands which separates the Caribbean Sea from the Atlantic Ocean. These islands became colonies of the major European powers in the 16th to the 18th centuries.

DEFINE THE FOLLOWING, USING THE DICTIONARY IF NECESSARY

acrimonious
altruism
axiomatic
county palatine
ethnocentricity
forager
Moslem
proselytizer
serf
supercargo

SAMPLE QUESTIONS

MULTIPLE CHOICE

1. The prosperity of Jamestown was insured by:
   a. the discovery of gold.
   b. the development of fur trading.
   c. financial support by the king.
   d. the cultivation of tobacco.

2. The chief difference between the "Puritans" and the "Separatists" was that:
   a. the Puritans sought to purify the Anglican Church; the Separatists thought it too corrupt to salvage.
   b. the Puritans thought the Anglican Church too "popish;" the Separatists thought it not "popish" enough.
   c. the Puritans favored the higher clergy; the Separatists opposed them.
   d. there was no real difference.

3. The House of Burgesses was to Virginia as the General Court was to:
   a. Rhode Island.
   b. Connecticut.
   c. Massachusetts.
   d. New York.

4. Which of the following did not originate as a company owned colony?
   a. Massachusetts.
   b. New York.
   c. Virginia.

d. Maryland.

5. Who of the following did not move from the Massachusetts Bay colony to found a new colony?
   a. John Winthrop.
   b. Thomas Hooker.
   c. Roger Williams.
   d. Anne Hutchinson.

TRUE-FALSE

1. The Massachusetts Bay colony favored religious toleration.

2. Colonial Georgia was valued by England as a buffer colony against Spanish Florida.

3. Captain John Smith and John Rolfe made important contributions toward the survival of Jamestown.

4. In English America, a proprietor was the owner of a joint-stock company.

5. Quakers settled chiefly in the colonies of New Jersey and Pennsylvania.

ANSWERS
MULTIPLE CHOICE: d,a,c,d,a. TRUE-FALSE: F,T,T,F,T.

The Thirteen Original Colonies

	Name	Founded by	When	Charter	Made Royal	1775 Status
1.	Virginia	London Co.	1607	1606 1609 1612	1624	Royal
	Plymouth	Separatists	1620	None		(Merged with Mass., 1691)
	Maine	F. Gorges	1623	1639		(Bought by Mass., 1677)
2.	New Hampshire	John Mason and others	1622	1679	1679	Royal (absorbed by Mass., 1641-1679)
3.	Massachusetts	Puritans	1630	1629	1691	Royal
4.	Maryland	Lord Baltimore	1634	1632	____	Proprietary
5.	Connecticut	Mass. emigrants	1636	1662	____	Self-governing
6.	Rhode Island	R. Williams	1636	1644 1663	____	Self-governing
	New Haven	Mass. emigrants	1638	None		(Merged with Conn., 1662)
7.	N. Carolina	Virginians	1653	1663	1729	Royal (separated informally from S.C., 1691)
8.	New York	Dutch Duke of York	1624 1664	1664	1685	Royal
9.	New Jersey	Berkeley and Carteret	1664	None	1702	Royal
10.	S. Carolina	Eight nobles	1670	1663	1729	Royal (separated formally from N.C., 1712)
11.	Pennsylvania	William Penn	1681	1681	____	Proprietary
12.	Delaware	Swedes	1638	None	____	Proprietary (merged with Penn., 1682, same governor, but separate assembly, granted 1703)
13.	Georgia	Oglethorpe and others	1733	1732	1752	Royal

2
The Colonial World

CHAPTER CHECKLIST

AMERICAN NATIONAL CHARACTER

Most Americans were originally colonizers from Europe, but they, and certainly their descendants, developed different characteristics. In particular they became self-reliant, individualistic, and accustomed to violence. The chief reason for the transformation was geography, their physical surroundings. Americans were isolated from Europe by the Atlantic Ocean. In addition, the North American continent was sparsely populated, which meant that most settlers could optimistically hope to own their own land, but at the same time must supply all their own needs. Geography at times inhibited the American, such as the Appalachian mountain range which kept the early colonials close to the coast.

LAND, LABOR AND TRADE

headright system. Originally used in Virginia, this system of land distribution provided that any person who transported himself to Virginia and remained 3 years could receive 50 acres for every dependent or servant he brought to America. The headright system prevailed throughout the South as well as in Pennsylvania and New Jersey.

quitrent. A fixed annual rent or land tax that "quit" or freed the landholder from feudal obligations to his lord, who was often the proprietor of the colony. Medieval in origin, this tax was unpopular and was effectively collected only in Maryland.

indentured servant system. Immigrants to the colonies paid for their passage by selling their future labor for a period of about 5 years. The indentured servant signed on with a ship captain who in turn sold him to an American buyer who wanted his labor and the 50-acre "headright."

Negro slaves. Introduced in English America by a Dutch ship at Jamestown in 1619. The first slaves may have eventually been freed just as indentured servants were, but by the mid 1600's, the institution of permanent slavery was firmly established. Relatively few Negroes were imported until the late 1600's, however, even in the southern colonies.

squatters. Individuals who settled on unclaimed land on the frontier without paying for it. When someone else wanted to establish legal title to the area, they often cried for "squatters' rights," the privilege of buying the land at the price it would have sold for originally, before they had made improvements on it.

multiangular trade. Describes the trade routes primarily between the colonies and England. One of the most profitable routes, known as the triangular trade, ran between Africa, the West Indian islands, and the ports of New York and Boston. Slaves were acquired in Africa and taken to the West Indies to work on sugar plantations. Molasses was picked up there and taken to Massachusetts to be made into rum. Rum was then shipped to Africa to be traded for slaves. Note the map on p. 45.

township system. A method of land settlement used in New England. The colonial government granted land in 36-square-mile blocks called townships to groups of settlers. This pattern provided for the orderly expansion of settlement in a basically urban rather than rural environment.

RELIGION

Puritans. A religious group, followers of the teachings of John Calvin, who wanted to purify the Church of England of its remaining Roman Catholic traditions. The predominant sect in New England was Puritan Congregationalist, so-called because in church government the local congregation was autonomous. The Puritans believed in predestination, that is, God had foreordained, even before one was born, whether a person was going to heaven. The Puritans searched for a sign that they were among "the elect," and good behavior along with material wealth were considered indications. The Puritans also valued education so that all would learn to read the Bible.

1662, Half-Way Covenant. A rule in Puritan Massachusetts which allowed grandchildren of full church members to be baptized, even though the children's parents were not full members of the church. The individuals who had been baptized, but had not had a religious "experience" which qualified them for full church membership, were called "half-way" members and were allowed to vote in civil elections.

Great Awakening. A religious movement of the 1740's which

featured an emotional rather than an intellectual approach to religion.

Jonathan Edwards (1703-1758). A Puritan minister famous for his emotional and vivid descriptions of eternal damnation, particularly in a 1741 sermon entitled "Sinners in the Hands of an Angry God." He later became a missionary among the Indians and then president of the College of New Jersey, now Princeton. Note his picture on p. 52.

George Whitefield (1715-1770). An English minister who made several speaking tours in the colonies during the Great Awakening, preaching very dramatic sermons which were particularly well-received in the frontier regions and in the south.

CONFLICTS WITHIN THE COLONIES

1676, Bacon's Rebellion. A protest led by the Virginia landowner Nathaniel Bacon against the Indian policies of Governor Berkeley. Bacon and his frontiersmen wanted a more aggressive policy against the Indian attacks and marched to Jamestown to demand it. During the rebellion Bacon died, and later Berkeley executed 22 of his followers.

1763, Paxton Boys. Frontiersmen in Pennsylvania who protested eastern indifference to Indian attacks by raiding an Indian village and then marching on Philadelphia where they were talked out of attacking the town by a delegation led by Benjamin Franklin.

1771, Regulators. A band of North Carolina frontiersmen who protested eastern domination of the colony and were militarily suppressed by government troops.

OTHER TERMS TO IDENTIFY

William Byrd (1674-1744). A wealthy Virginia landowner who was equally adept at growing tobacco, prospecting for ore, serving in the House of Burgesses, and collecting a large library.

1763, Parson's Cause. A lawsuit involving the payment of the Anglican clergy in Virginia. In principle the suit questioned the right of the Privy Council to disallow, or veto, a colonial law. Patrick Henry effectively spoke for the Virginia colonists and against the clergy and the Council.

1636, Harvard. The oldest college in English America, founded by the Puritans primarily as a training school for Congregational ministers. The college, located in Cambridge, Massachusetts, was named after John Harvard, who in 1638 bequeathed his library and half his estate to the new institution.

Reverend Cotton Mather (1663-1728). A leading Puritan clergyman in Massachusetts who wrote over 450 books on religion and science. One of his books was on witchcraft, and some believe it contributed to the Salem witchhunt in 1692. Mather also helped introduce smallpox innoculation in America.

GLOSSARY

Arminianism. The religious doctrines of Jacobus Arminius (1560-1609), a Dutch Protestant theologian who opposed John Calvin's doctrine of predestination. He placed more emphasis on free will and the importance of good works in obtaining salvation.

chattel. An article of personal, movable property; a term often used to refer to a slave.

Enlightenment. An 18th century philosophical movement concerned with critically examining previously accepted doctrines. Scholars of the Enlightenment placed much faith in the power of human reasoning to understand the universe and devoted much time to collecting data about the world around them. The varied contributions of Benjamin Franklin and Thomas Jefferson are examples of the influence of the Englightenment in America.

established church. A church officially recognized by the government and supported as a state institution. In the southern colonies this term usually referred to the Church of England.

Glorious Revolution. In 1688 James II, a Catholic, was forced to vacate the throne of England and flee to France. His Protestant daughter, Mary, and her husband, William, were offered the throne but only after they promised certain rights to Parliament. This bloodless "revolution" marks a turning point in Parliament's power versus that of the Crown.

gristmill. A mill for grinding grain.

guinea. A British gold coin, no longer in use, which was worth one pound and one shilling. (1 shilling= 1/20 of a pound). It was originally made of gold from the Guinea coast of Africa.

naval stores. Timber byproducts such as turpentine or pitch, the latter originally used to make the seams of wooden ships watertight.

"peculiar institution". A term often used by southerners to

refer to slavery.

£. The symbol for the pound, the basic monetary unit of Great Britain.

Protectorate. A period in British history (1649-1660) during which Oliver Cromwell served as Lord Protector.

Saint Lawrence River. The river which is the outlet of the Great Lakes and links them to the Atlantic. This long water passage was a highway for French explorers, fur traders, and missionaries into the interior.

Scotch-Irish. Scots, living in Ireland, who moved on to America. In the early 1600's James I, to further the conquest of Catholic Ireland, had moved Presbyterian Scots to the northern Irish county of Ulster. But 100 years later, these Scotch-Irish, or Scots living in northern Ireland, were persecuted. They were not allowed to export their woolens, they were forced to conform their religious practices to those of the Anglican Church, and as their long-term leases expired, they were forced to pay higher rent on their farmland. Instead of signing new leases, many Scotch-Irish moved to the American frontier where some of them fought the Indians just as they had fought the Irish.

snuff. A preparation of finely pulverized tobacco that can be drawn up into the nostrils by inhaling.

DEFINE THE FOLLOWING, USING THE DICTIONARY IF NECESSARY

bibliophile
clique
demographic
disparate
hierarchy
invidious
lascivious
pyrotechnics
resin
scions

SAMPLE QUESTIONS

MULTIPLE CHOICE

1. A headright was:
   a. a grant of land to anyone who paid his own or someone else's passage to America.
   b. a person who worked for another in America in exchange for payment of his passage.
   c. a yearly tax paid to a proprietor.
   d. a curse supposedly placed by witches on young girls in Salem.

2. Under the indenture system, the servant was bound for:

a. a year.
b. approximately five years.
c. life.
d. until he could purchase his freedom.

3. Which of the following was not a minister of the Great Awakening?
   a. Jonathan Edwards.
   b. Increase Mather.
   c. George Whitefield.
   d. James Oglethorpe.

4. Which one of the following is not an example of western frontiersmen protesting eastern domination of their colony?
   a. Bacon's Rebellion: Virginia.
   b. Paxton Boys: Pennsylvania.
   c. Regulators: North Carolina.
   d. Glorious Revolution: Massachusetts.

5. The American national characteristics of self-reliance and individualism are primarily a result of:
   a. European heritage.
   b. African influence.
   c. American geography.
   d. French Canadian influence.

TRUE-FALSE

1. The Enlightenment was a period characterized by an emotional approach to religion.

2. Newer western counties in the colonies were sometimes denied equal representation in the colonial legislatures.

3. Rice and indigo were important crops raised in the New England colonies.

4. The established church in the southern colonies was the Anglican Church.

5. All of the colonies established modest property qualifications for voting.

ANSWERS
MULTIPLE CHOICE: a,b,d,d,c. TRUE-FALSE: F,T,F,T,F.

3

America and the British Empire

CHAPTER CHECKLIST

GOVERNMENT AND TRADE

Comparison of Governments

England	English Colonies	United States After 1789
King	Governor	President
Parliament		Congress
House of Lords	Governor's Council	Senate
House of Commons	Assembly	House of Representatives

Privy Council. A group of advisers to the Crown who established colonial policy. They could disallow or annul colonial laws and served as the court of last appeal in colonial disputes.

Board of Trade. Established in England in 1696, it nominated governors and other high officials for royal colonies and reviewed laws passed by colonial legislatures. The Board recommended to the Privy Council which laws should be disallowed. In order to influence the decisions of the Board of Trade the colonies maintained agents, or lobbyists, in London, the most famous of whom was Benjamin Franklin.

mercantilism. An economic theory which stated that a nation's wealth was based on the amount of gold and silver bullion in its treasury. There were several ways to achieve this wealth. One method was to own mines, such as those discovered by Spain in Mexico and South America. A second method was to acquire the bullion of other countries through trade. In order to do this, a country had to sell more to another country than it bought. This situation is referred to as "maintaining a favorable balance of trade." Note that a favorable balance meant that there was no balance; instead a country wanted to export more than it imported.

Colonies were considered very important in the mercantilistic scheme because they could yield raw materials and also provide markets for manufactured products of the mother country. For example, England could buy lumber from the New England colonies rather than from a European country. Purchasing from a colony enabled England to keep her bullion within the empire, because the colony was considered as simply an extension of the mother country.

Navigation Acts. A series of acts beginning in 1650 to regulate the commerce of the British Empire. Most important, all trade of the colonies had to be carried in English ships, which meant that all European products destined for America went to England first and were then reloaded.

enumerated articles. As part of the Navigation Acts, certain products earmarked as articles which could only be traded within the British Empire. In 1660 they included sugar, tobacco, cotton, ginger, and dyes like indigo (blue) and fustic (yellow). In the early 1700's rice, molasses, naval stores, furs, and copper were included.

"salutary neglect." A term used by Sir Robert Walpole (1676-1745), a British politician, in referring to the fact that England often looked the other way when Americans violated the Navigation Acts. Walpole felt that the absence of overly strict enforcement was probably healthy, or "salutary."

1756-1763, Great War for the Empire.

--Called the Seven Years War in Europe. It was the fourth in a series of wars in which England opposed France.
--Called the French and Indian War in America. English colonists fought the French and their Indian allies.
--Campaigns took place in the Ohio Valley, where young George Washington made several unsuccessful expeditions to the area of Fort Duquesne, now Pittsburgh.
--Another campaign area was Canada. Quebec fell to the British when the English General Wolfe defeated the French forces under General Montcalm.
--1763, Treaty of Paris. Great Britain acquired Canada and the eastern half of the Mississippi Valley, thus ending the French threat in North America.
--In other treaties, Spain acquired New Orleans and the Louisiana Territory from France, and England temporarily acquired Florida.

ENGLAND TIGHTENS CONTROLS

Proclamation of 1763. A declaration that no colonists were to cross the Appalachian Mountain range to settle. British officials hoped to check westward expansion and keep the colonies more closely tied to England, and in addition they hoped to pacify the Indians by helping them retain their lands. Note the map on p. 79.

1764, Sugar Act. Among the first acts passed by Parliament for the specific purpose of raising money in the colonies rather than simply regulating trade. The law placed tariffs, or import taxes, on sugar, coffee, wines, and other products. Taxes on European products imported by way of Great Britain were doubled, and the enumerated articles list was extended to include iron, raw silk, potash, and other items. Much emphasis was placed on enforcing the Sugar Act, and those accused of violating it were to be tried before British naval officers.

1764, Currency Act. Forbade the colonies to issue any more paper money. It was designed to prevent the colonists from paying creditors with depreciated money.

1765, Stamp Act. A tax on colonial newspapers, legal documents, licenses, and other printed matter. The colonists opposed it because it was a direct, internal tax, not a tax on trade within the Empire. The colonists protested in several ways:

--Intercolonial Stamp Act Congress met in New York to protest taxation without representation.
--An organization, the Sons of Liberty, staged demonstrations against the tax.
--Colonists not only refused to use the stamps, which would show that they had paid the tax, but they also boycotted other British goods.

1766. Stamp Act repealed. On the same day, Parliament passed the Declaratory Act, which stated that the colonies were "subordinate" and that Parliament could enact any law it wished to govern them.

DIFFERING INTERPRETATIONS OF CONCEPTS

Representation.

--Virtual representation. The belief that every member of Parliament represented everyone in the British Empire, not just his own district. Even today an MP (Member of Parliament) does not have to live in the district from which he is elected.
--Direct representation. The belief in America that members of the colonial assemblies represented the people of the district in which they ran for office.

Constitution.

--To Englishmen, the constitution meant the sum total of laws, traditions, and judicial decisions which had developed over the centuries and which governed the country.

The British Constitution is considered flexible in that it can be changed by an act of Parliament or a judicial decision.

--To Americans, a constitution meant a written charter, similar to those granted to the colonies. The present United States Constitution, adopted in 1789, is considered rigid, because it is above the ordinary laws of the land and can only be amended by a specially prescribed procedure, that is, a two-thirds vote in each house of Congress, and ratification by three-fourths of the states.

Sovereignty.

--The English believed that ultimate political power, or sovereignty, could not be divided. After the Glorious Revolution of 1688, Parliament was considered sovereign.

--Americans developed ideas about divisions of power, that is, that their own colonial assemblies, rather than Parliament, should have the final say concerning certain local matters.

CONTROLS AND PROTESTS

1767, Townshend Acts. A series of levies or taxes on glass, lead, paints, paper, and tea imported into the colonies. The acts were named after Charles Townshend, who was chancellor of the exchequer, a position similar to today's Secretary of the Treasury in the United States. Colonists protested in various ways:

--A boycott of British products was established.

--A "Circular Letter" (1768) was sent out by the Massachusetts General Court, asking other colonies what action should be taken.

--John Dickinson published Letters From a Farmer in Pennsylvania to the Inhabitants of the British Colonies, questioning the right of Parliament to tax the colonies.

1770. Townshend duties, except for a threepenny tax on tea, were repealed.

1770, Boston Massacre. Townspeople taunted British troops at the Custom House and when reinforcements were called in they fired into the crowd killing five Boston citizens. Propagandists called it a massacre and played up the event in the local press. See the engraving on p. 89.

1772, Gaspee incident. The Gaspee, a British patrol boat, ran aground in Rhode Island while pursuing a suspected smuggler. Local people boarded the Gaspee, wounded the commander, and set fire to the ship. When the British tried to bring the culprits to justice they could find no one to testify against them. This incident strengthened British conviction that the colonists were lawless.

1773, Boston Tea Party. The Tea Act of 1773 gave a monopoly on tea to the British East India Company, granting them the privilege of bypassing middlemen and selling tea directly to favored colonial merchants. The threepenny tax on tea from the Townshend duties remained. In Boston, local Sons of Liberty refused to let the tea be unloaded and taxed by thinly disguising themselves as Indians, boarding the ships, and dumping the tea chests into Boston harbor.

1774, Coercive Acts. Three acts applying to Massachusetts, passed by Parliament in retaliation for the Boston Tea Party.

--Boston Port Act. Closed Boston harbor until citizens paid for tea.
--Administration of Justice Act. Court cases could be transferred outside of Massachusetts if the governor felt an impartial trial was unlikely.
--Massachusetts Government Act. Revised the colony's charter, giving more power to the royally appointed governor and making the governor's council appointive rather than elective, among other changes weakening local authority.

1774, First Continental Congress. Met in Philadelphia with all colonies but Georgia sending delegates. It passed a resolution claiming for the colonial assemblies exclusive power of legislation, subject only to royal veto. The congress was an "extralegal," that is, unofficial, body which met to discuss common concerns.

"Continental Association." The delegates at the Continental Congress organized an "Association" to boycott all British goods and to stop all exports to the empire. Local committees were appointed to enforce the boycott, by force if necessary.

OTHER TERMS TO IDENTIFY

William Pitt (1708-1778). British minister whose strategies contributed to English victory over France in the Seven Years War. See the map entitled "Pitt's Strategy, The French and Indian War, 1758-1760" on p. 76.

George Grenville (1712-1770). Prime Minister of England (1763-1765) who initiated a policy to get the colonies to help pay off the tremendous war debt which England had acquired during the Seven Years War.

John Locke (1632-1704). A British political philosopher whose Two Treatises of Government (1690) was influential in American thought before the independence movement. Locke stated that originally men had lived in a state of nature and enjoyed complete liberty, but then had set up government to protect their "natural rights," particularly the ownership of private property. He further stated, "If any one shall claim a power to lay and levy taxes on the people by his own authority, and without such consent of the people, he thereby invades the fundamental law of property, and subverts the end of government." According to Locke, if a government exceeded its rightful powers, people could then cease to obey it, and establish another government.

Samuel Adams (1722-1803). A Massachusetts patriot, second cousin of John Adams, who fanned the flames of the independence movement. He helped organize the Sons of Liberty and instigated the Boston Tea Party. In 1776 he signed the Declaration of Independence, and later became governor of Massachusetts from 1793 to 1797. Note his portrait on p. 88.

1774, Intolerable Acts. A term used by the Americans to refer to the three Coercive Acts plus a new Quartering Act and the Quebec Act. This legislation directly contributed to the outbreak of the revolutionary movement.

GLOSSARY

ad hoc. A Latin phrase meaning for a specific purpose, case, or situation. For example, an ad hoc committee deals with a specific problem or project.

bullion. Gold or silver in the form of bars, ingots, or plates.

common law. The system of law used in England and countries colonized by England. Its distinctive feature is that it represents the law of the courts as expressed in judicial decisions. The grounds for deciding cases are found in precedents provided by past decisions, as contrasted to the Civil Law system, based on statutes, that is, laws passed by a legislature. In reality a combination of both are used today because with rapidly changing conditions there is often no judicial precedent and statutes have become more important.

El Dorado. A mythical place in Spanish America rich in precious metals and jewels, sought by 16th century explorers. Originally the term meant "the gilded man" and referred to a tradition in Colombia that an Indian chief covered himself with gold dust as an offering to the gods and then bathed in Lake Guatavita, washing the precious metal into the water.

French West Indies. The islands of Guadeloupe, Martinique, and what is today Haiti, in the Caribbean Sea.

nouveau riche. A French term meaning new rich or one who has recently become wealthy. The term is often used critically to imply showiness or ostentation.

raw materials. Unprocessed natural products used in manufacturing. The English colonies provided such raw materials as lumber and naval stores.

DEFINE THE FOLLOWING, USING THE DICTIONARY IF NECESSARY

accretion
ambiguous
anomalous
aphorism
complacency
fallacy
inexorably
pragmatist
recalcitrant
stoically

SAMPLE QUESTIONS

MULTIPLE CHOICE

1. By the end of the colonial period most of the British colonies in America were governed by:
   a. the elders of the established church.
   b. a governor, council, and assembly, all elected by the people.
   c. a governor and council appointed by the king, and an assembly elected by the voters.
   d. the appointed representatives of the companies which had established the colonies.

2. The Proclamation of 1763:
   a. called for colonial enlistments to put down the Pontiac Rebellion.
   b. prohibited settlers from crossing the Appalachians.
   c. granted an extensive tract to the Ohio Company.
   d. prohibited colonial paper money.

3. England felt that Americans had parliamentary representation because:
   a. Americans had delegates in the House of Commons.
   b. the colonies had their own assemblies.
   c. the members of the House of Commons represented all citizens.
   d. the colonies were represented in the Continental Congress.

4. After the Boston Tea Party of 1773, the British:
   a. closed the port of Boston.
   b. repealed the tax on tea.
   c. banned the importing of coffee.
   d. summoned the First Continental Congress into session.

5. The First Continental Congress met to:
   a. declare war on England.
   b. protest the Coercive Acts.

c. adopt the Declaration of Independence.
d. protest the Stamp Act.

TRUE-FALSE

1. Under mercantilism, a colony was valuable if it produced the same manufactured products as the mother country.

2. Restrictions on paper money and restrictions on colonial manufacturing were causes of discontent throughout the colonies.

3. The Declaratory Act of 1766 asserted the right of Parliament to legislate for the colonies.

4. The Stamp Act was repealed by Congress.

5. The *Gaspee* incident strengthened British conviction that the colonists were lawless.

ANSWERS
MULTIPLE CHOICE: c,b,c,a,b. TRUE-FALSE: F,T,T,F,T.

Portfolio 2

Benjamin Franklin

CHECKLIST OF DATES AND EVENTS

--1706. Born in Boston.
--Influenced by the ideas of the Enlightenment which had spread to America.
--Became a printer, and then publisher of the Pennsylvania Gazette and Poor Richard's Almanac.
--Conducted experiments with a kite to prove that electricity and lightning were one and the same. Invented the lightning rod.
--Invented the Franklin stove, bifocal glasses, and a copying machine, among other products.
--1727. Helped establish the Junto, a debating society, out of which grew a library and a fire company for Philadelphia.
--1743-1744. Helped set up the American Philosophical Society, which is still in existence today.
--1751. Helped found the academy which later became the University of Pennsylvania.
--1753. Appointed as His Majesty's Deputy Postmaster General for all of North America.
--1754. Presented the Albany Plan of Union to the delegates of seven colonies who were meeting in Albany, New York, to make an agreement with the Iroquois Indians. The plan called for an intercolonial defense council with the power to tax, raise an army and construct fortifications, and purchase Indian lands for western settlement. A Crown-appointed official with veto power would preside. But Franklin was ahead of his time in trying to get the colonies to work together, and the plan was rejected by the individual colonial assemblies as well as by the Crown.
--A member of the Pennsylvania assembly.
--Served as a colonial agent in London.
--1763-1764. Urged calling out troops to defend Philadelphia against the 500 frontier Paxton Boys marching on it.
--1765-1766. Mildly opposed to the Stamp Act at first and then actively campaigned to get the House of Commons to repeal it.
--1775. Represented Pennsylvania at the Second Continental Congress which met in Philadelphia. One of his committee assignments was to help draft the Declaration of Inde-

pendence.
--1778. Concluded a treaty of alliance with France.
--1782-1783. Negotiated a peace treaty with England, the 1783 Peace of Paris.
--1785. Became governor of Pennsylvania.
--1787. Represented Pennsylvania at the Constitutional Convention.
--1790. Died in Philadelphia at age 83.

GLOSSARY

Prometheus. In Greek mythology, a god who stole fire from Olympus, the mountain where the gods lived, and gave it to humans in order to improve their lives.

odometer. An instrument that indicates distance traveled by a vehicle. Franklin worked out ideas for an odometer.

unclubbed hair. Loose flowing hair, not pulled back into what today would be called a pony tail. Franklin wore his hair long and unclubbed.

tallow chandler. A person who makes and sells candles. Franklin's father was a chandler.

journeyman. One who has fully served his apprenticeship in a trade or craft and is a qualified worker in another's employ. Franklin moved to Philadelphia to seek work as a journeyman printer.

Wedgwood. A type of pottery or china made by Josiah Wedgwood (1730-1795) and his successors. The most typical examples are figures which stand out in white relief on an unglazed blue background. Note the picture of a Wedgwood medallion on the first page of Portfolio 2.

E Pluribus Unum. A Latin phrase meaning "from many, one." This phrase was the motto of the new nation.

DEFINE THE FOLLOWING, USING THE DICTIONARY IF NECESSARY

acerbic	epitome
allegory	hypothesis
effulgence	meteorology

4

The American Revolution

CHAPTER CHECKLIST

STEPS TOWARD A FINAL BREAK

April 19, 1775: Lexington and Concord. Towns in Massachusetts where the first real skirmishes of the Revolutionary War took place. General Thomas Gage, commander in chief of British forces in North America and also governor of Massachusetts, ordered troops to Concord to destroy a stockpile of arms which the Patriots had been accumulating. Paul Revere and others spread the warning, and when the Redcoats passed through Lexington on the way to Concord they found about 70 Minute Men occupying the common. Gunfire was exchanged and 8 were killed. The British proceeded to Boston, and were harassed by sniper fire all along the road. April 19th is considered the first day of the Revolutionary War.

May 10, 1775: Second Continental Congress. Convened in Philadelphia. John Hancock, a Boston merchant, was elected president of the Congress, which included delegates from all the colonies. Some had attended the First Continental Congress as well. The Congress appointed George Washington of Virginia as Commander in Chief of the Continental Army and then turned to the task of recruiting men and obtaining supplies.

June, 1775: Battle of Bunker Hill. Also fought on nearby Breed's Hill in Charlestown, Massachusetts, near Boston. General Gage's troops succeeded in pushing the Patriots from the area but paid a terrible toll, losing 1,000 men compared to the Patriots' 400. The battle is significant because after so much bloodshed the prospect of a negotiated settlement was greatly reduced.

January, 1776: Common Sense. An essay by Thomas Paine which was very effective in swaying public opinion toward a complete break with England. Paine attacked the whole concept of an hereditary monarchy as being a corrupt institution and called King George III a "Royal

Brute."

July 4, 1776: Declaration of Independence. Adopted by the Continental Congress. The document was primarily written by Thomas Jefferson, with additions by Benjamin Franklin and John Adams. The Declaration was in two parts. The first part tried to justify the Americans' right to revolt and was based on the ideas of John Locke. The second listed particular grievances against George III. Many Americans had blamed Parliament for the colonies' problems but had remained loyal to the Crown. This section of the document tried to personally indict the King.

Tory. An American who remained loyal to England during the Revolutionary War, also called Loyalist. Tories included Anglican clergymen, merchants with ties to England, and rural elements in New York and North Carolina who resented the leadership within their own colonies. Between 7.6 and 18 per cent of the white population were Tories, and about 100,000 left the United States after the war to move to other British possessions. Tories got their name from the English political party which traditionally supported a strong monarchy rather than a strong parliament. The American Tories remained loyal to George III, King of England.

1776. Framing of new constitutions by the states which generally based these documents on their colonial charters. Most had an executive or governor, with weak powers, and a strong representative legislature, elected primarily by male property owners.

THE CONDUCT OF WAR AND PEACE

October, 1777: Battle of Saratoga. A Patriot victory in New York in which General Burgoyne surrendered with 5,700 troops. Note the map "Saratoga and Philadelphia Campaigns 1777" on p. 110. The significance of the victory is that it sufficiently impressed France so that she diplomatically recognized the United States and signed a formal treaty of alliance.

February, 1778: Alliance with France. France recognized the United States as being independent and signed a military alliance and commercial treaty with the new nation. Shortly thereafter France declared war on England. The treaty establishing the alliance was drafted by the French Foreign Minister, the Compte de Vergennes, and by the American commissioners in Paris, Benjamin Franklin, Arthur Lee, and Silas Deane.

1777-1778, Valley Forge. An area in Pennsylvania where Washington's Continental Army spent a terrible winter. The troops suffered from lack of food, clothing, and military supplies, and a number of them went home or signed up with the British. Valley Forge was considered a low point in the war for the Americans.

<u>1781, Yorktown</u>. Washington's troops and a French fleet trapped General Cornwallis at Yorktown, Virginia, and forced him to surrender in October, 1781. This victory was the last major battle of the war. See the map "Yorktown and the War in the South" on p. 114.

<u>1777-1789, Articles of Confederation</u>. Were proposed in 1777, finally ratified by all the states in 1781, and in force until the Constitution went into effect in 1789. The Articles gave a legal basis to the powers the Continental Congress had already been exercising. The individual states were considered independent and sovereign, and each state had one vote in the Congress, although they could send more representatives. A unanimous vote was required to pass most legislation. Under the Articles, the Congress could support the Army, conduct foreign relations, borrow money from foreign powers, and ask the states to contribute money. But the Congress could not tax, regulate domestic or foreign commerce, or enforce its authority.

<u>1783, Peace of Paris</u>.

--Negotiated primarily by Benjamin Franklin and John Jay.
--Ended the Revolutionary War.
--England recognized United States as an independent country.
--Boundaries set at Great Lakes to the north, Mississippi River to the west, and northern border of Florida to the South.
--United States sailors could fish off of Newfoundland and dry their catch on beaches of Labrador and Nova Scotia.
--Congress would "recommend" that confiscated Tory property be returned and would prevent further seizures.
--Congress agreed not to impede British creditors from collecting their debts.

WESTERN LAND

<u>1785, Land Ordinance</u>. Provided for surveying the Western territories so that they could be sold by the national government. The land was divided into six-mile-square townships, and further subdivided into 36 sections of 640 acres each. The land was to be sold at auction at a minimum price of one dollar an acre, and the money went into the national treasury. The 16th section of each township was earmarked for maintaining a school.

<u>1787, Northwest Ordinance</u>. Established a plan for setting up governments in the western territories so that they could eventually join the Union on an equal footing with the original thirteen. This ordinance specifically referred to the Northwest Territory, an area bounded by the Ohio River, the Mississippi River, and the Great Lakes, which was to be carved into 3 to 5 states. Note

the map entitled "The United States 1787" on p. 119.

When the territory opened, a governor and three judges were appointed by Congress. After 5,000 adult males moved to the area the people (adult males) could elect an assembly and send a nonvoting delegate to Congress, although the governor retained veto power over the assembly. When 60,000 persons moved into one of the political subdivisions, that area could draft a constitution, submit it to Congress for approval, and become a state. Its constitution had to provide for a republican, that is, an elected, representative government; and it had to prohibit slavery.

OTHER TERMS TO IDENTIFY

Minute Men. The local volunteer units in the Revolutionary War who were to be ready to protect their communities against the British at a moment's notice.

Paul Revere (1735-1818). A Boston silversmith who made a famous horseback ride on April 18, 1775 to warn Massachusetts villagers between Boston and Concord that the British troops were coming. In fact, Revere was captured in Lexington, and Dr. Samuel Prescott carried the message to Concord, but Revere's ride is well-known because of a poem written in 1861 by Henry Wadsworth Longfellow entitled "Paul Revere's Ride."

Hessian soldiers. Professional soldiers, or mercenaries, hired by the British to fight in America. They were from the German province of Hesse.

John Dickinson (1732-1808). A Patriot who was considered a conservative leader because he favored reconciliation rather than revolt. He expressed this view in the Letters From A Farmer in Pennsylvania, published in 1767-1768. After hostilities broke out, he helped draft the Articles of Confederation, and was later a delegate from Delaware to the 1787 Constitutional Convention.

Benedict Arnold (1741-1801). A Revolutionary general who participated in a number of successful campaigns against the British. But in 1780, as commander at West Point, New York, he plotted to turn that site over to the British in exchange for a sum of money and a commission in the British army. The plot was discovered and Arnold escaped before being captured. The following year he participated in several British raids against Americans and then went into exile in Canada and England.

Robert Morris (1734-1806). A Philadelphia merchant who was appointed by Congress to be superintendent of finances from 1781 to 1784. He reorganized part of the supply system for the army, set up a National Bank of North

America, and got the country back on a specie basis, that is, using coined money rather than the worthless paper notes which had led to the saying "not worth a Continental."

GLOSSARY

First Lord of the Admiralty. Head of the British navy.

John Bull. A character often used in 18th and 19th century cartoons to represent England. Note the captions by the pictures on pp. P2-XXI and 111. He might be compared to today's Uncle Sam as a symbol of the United States.

livre. A unit of French money which is no longer used. It was originally worth one pound of silver.

minister plenipotentiary. A rank in the diplomatic corps. This title is used for one ranking between a minister and an ambassador. For example, in 1779 John Adams was appointed by the Continental Congress as minister plenipotentiary to conduct peace negotiations in Europe.

redoubt. A small, often temporary defensive fortification. For example, the Patriots constructed a redoubt on Breed's Hill in 1775, which was overrun by the British.

town common. A tract of land belonging to or used by the community as a whole. It was frequently used in New England villages to pasture animals.

DEFINE THE FOLLOWING, USING THE DICTIONARY IF NECESSARY

demagogue
feinting
ice floes
ignominious
locus
moribund
paean
prorogue

SAMPLE QUESTIONS

MULTIPLE CHOICE

1. Samuel Adams, John Hancock, and Patrick Henry were all:
   a. Tories
   b. Governors appointed by King George III.
   c. involved in the Boston Tea Party.
   d. Patriots

2. General Gage sent troops to Lexington and Concord because:
   a. he learned of the storage of a large amount of gunpowder there.
   b. he wished to provoke a colonial attack.
   c. the colonists were not paying the tax on tea.
   d. he wanted to stop Paul Revere.

3. The pamphlet written to demonstrate to the colonists the advantages of separation from England was called:
   a. Exposition and Protest.
   b. New Freedom.
   c. The Federalist Papers.
   d. Common Sense.

4. One of the important powers which Congress lacked under the Articles of Confederation was the power to:
   a. regulate interstate trade.
   b. borrow money.
   c. make treaties.
   d. declare war.

5. How did England's administration of her colonies before the American Revolution <u>differ</u> from American administration of western territorial dependencies following the American Revolution?
   a. the authority of England as a central government was represented by a governor.
   b. the English colonies were subject to taxation by the mother country.
   c. England granted virtually no self-government to her colonies.
   d. England viewed the colonies as perpetual dependencies of the mother country.

TRUE-FALSE

1. Tories were Americans who were ready to defend their communities against the British at a minute's notice.

2. Many Anglican clergymen remained loyal to King George during the Revolution.

3. The last major battle of the Revolution took place at Saratoga.

4. The Land Ordinance of 1785 set up a government for the Northwest Territory.

5. <u>E Pluribus Unum</u> is the motto of the United States.

ANSWERS
<u>MULTIPLE</u> CHOICE: d,a,d,a,d. TRUE-FALSE: F,T,F,F,T.

5

Nationalism Triumphant

CHAPTER CHECKLIST

PROBLEMS THE CONFEDERATION COULD NOT SOLVE

Threat to the West posed by Britain and Spain.

--Britain would not surrender seven military posts in the northwest, despite the Peace of Paris. Note the map "The United States 1787-1802" on p. 145.

--Spain periodically closed the lower Mississippi River to American commerce and denied the right to deposit goods at New Orleans while awaiting ocean going vessels.

Disruption of foreign commerce resulting from independence.

--United States was now outside of British empire, and under the rules of mercantilism, could no longer freely trade with her accustomed markets in England and British West Indies.

--A tariff, or tax on imports, might have helped American "infant" industries, but Congress did not have the power to pass such laws, and an attempted amendment to the Articles could not muster the unanimous vote required.

Collapse of the financial structure.

--Wartime inflation followed by postwar deflation.

--Stay laws. Laws which granted an extension to someone behind in paying off a debt. After the war many farmers pushed for the passage of "stay laws" to delay foreclosure on their farms. Foreclosure meant that their property was taken from them because of overdue debts or unpaid taxes.

--1786-1787, Shays' Rebellion. A revolt led by the revolutionary veteran, Daniel Shays, in Massachusetts. He and other small property holders banded together to intimidate or close down courts to prevent foreclosure action against debtors. He and his group were finally routed when they tried to take supplies from a Springfield, Massachusetts arsenal, and Shays escaped to Vermont. He was later pardoned.

STEPS TOWARD A NEW CONSTITUTION

<u>1785, Mount Vernon Conference</u>. Representatives of Virginia and Maryland met at Washington's Virginia estate, Mount Vernon, to discuss navigation on the Potomac River. They suggested a conference of all states to discuss common commercial problems.

<u>1786, Annapolis Conference</u>. Five states sent delegates to a conference at Annapolis, Maryland. One of the representatives, Alexander Hamilton of New York, suggested a meeting the following year in Philadelphia to propose changes to the Articles.

<u>1787, Philadelphia Convention</u>. All states except Rhode Island sent delegates to propose revisions of the Articles of Confederation, but instead they wrote an entirely new Constitution. Most of the delegates shared the following ideas:

--Federal system. That political power divided between the states and the national government.
--Republican government. Ultimate authority resided in the people and not in a monarch.
--Democracy. Government by the people, exercised either directly or through elected representatives.

CONSTITUTION

<u>Great Compromise</u>. A compromise between the large and small states concerning representation in the Congress. The large states had rallied behind the <u>Virginia Plan</u> whereas the smaller states supported the <u>New Jersey Plan</u>. The Great Compromise, sometimes called the Connecticut Compromise, provided for 2 houses in the Congress.

The House of Representatives was based on population and its members elected directly by the people for a two-year term. The Senate gave equal representation to each state, and each state's two members would be elected for six-year terms by the state legislatures. The 17th amendment (1913) provided that senators be elected directly by the people rather than by the state legislatures.

<u>Three-fifths Compromise</u>. Three-fifths of the total number of slaves in a state would be counted, both in determining representation in the House of Representatives and in deciding each state's share of direct federal taxes.

<u>Electoral College System.</u> The indirect method used to elect the President. Each state could choose a certain number of electors, equal to the total number of Senators and Representatives from that state. The electors then

voted for two persons for President. If no candidate got a majority, then the House of Representatives, each state casting one vote, could elect the President from the top five candidates. The runner-up became Vice President.

The system was slightly changed by the 12th Amendment in 1803. Since that time, the electors only vote for one candidate and if no one gets a majority, the President is selected from the top three by the members of the House. Balloting for Vice President is now done separately.

judicial review. The practice of the courts of declaring a law void if it conflicts with the Constitution, although such authority is not specifically granted by the Constitution.

checks and balances. Features in the Constitution designed to keep one area or branch of the government from becoming too powerful. For example, to become a law, a bill must get a majority vote in both houses of Congress and be signed by the President. But he can also veto it, and then it takes a two-thirds vote in each house to override the presidential veto. Another example involves the treaty-making power. The President or someone appointed by him can negotiate a treaty, but it must be ratified by a two-thirds vote of the Senate.

RATIFICATION CONTROVERSY

Federalists. People who favored ratification of the new Constitution. Nine of the thirteen states had to approve the document before it went into effect, as it did in 1789. In general, the Federalists tended to be professionals or merchants. Many were wealthy, involved in commerce, and interested in an efficient government.

Antifederalists. People who opposed ratification of the Constitution. Many were small farmers, debtors, and people who were wary of the power granted to the central government by the Constitution. They were afraid it would destroy the independence of the states.

1787-1788, Federalist Papers. A series of 85 essays written primarily by Alexander Hamilton, with about 28 by James Madison and by John Jay. The essays appeared as a series in New York newspapers under the pen name of "Publius" and were designed to win support for adoption of the Constitution.

1788. Constitution ratified by the necessary nine states and legally in effect.

1789. George Washington elected President by the Electoral College System and inaugurated in New York City, the first national capital.

1791, Bill of Rights. The first ten amendments of the Constitution. One of the criticisms of the Antifederalists had been that the Constitution made no provision for personal freedoms, and these amendments were designed in part to win their support. To amend the Constitution requires a two-thirds vote in each house and ratification by three-fourths of the states.

> GEORGE WASHINGTON (1732-1799), 1st President
>
> --Born in Virginia and worked as a surveyor.
> --Participated in several campaigns against the French in the Ohio Valley.
> --Delegate to the First and Second Continental Congresses.
> --Commander in Chief of the American armies in the Revolution.
> --Lived at his estate in Virginia called Mount Vernon.
> --President of the Philadelphia Convention which drafted the Constitution.
> --President (1789-1797).

HAMILTON AND THE TREASURY

Alexander Hamilton (1755-1804). Born in the British West Indies and emigrated to America in 1773 where he quickly became involved in the Revolutionary movement, and served as Washington's aide-de-camp (1777-1781). He was a New York delegate to the Constitutional Convention and worked for its adoption by writing most of the Federalist Papers. Hamilton was the first secretary of the treasury (1789-1795), a leader in the Federalist Party, and died in 1804 from wounds suffered in a duel with Aaron Burr.

funding of the national debt. The national government would recognize and pay in full all the "I.O.U.'s" which it had issued during the war to farmers, soldiers, and merchants in exchange for their produce and services, though many of these securities or notes were no longer in the hands of the original recipients.

For example, if a farmer had received a note for $100 during the war, he probably could not afford to wait to see if the government would eventually pay him. Instead, he sold it to a wealthy speculator for $75 in cash. When Hamilton decided to fund these securities or pay them off at par, that is, in full, these speculators received $100, although they had only paid $75 to the farmer.

assumption of state debts. Since the war had been fought to benefit the whole country, the national government would assume, or take over, all the debts incurred by the individual states during that time. This idea was opposed by most southern states because they had already paid off their debts. However, a settlement was reached in the Compromise of 1790 in which the state debts would be assumed, which would help the northern states, and in return, the permanent location of the national capital would be in the South on the Potomac River.

National Bank. Founded as a place where government income could be stored and from which government expenditures would be made. It also issued bank notes, which could serve as money. Hamilton's bank had a twenty-year charter and lasted from 1791 to 1811.

The National Bank, or the Bank of the United States as it was called, should not be confused with present-day national banks. The latter are so-called simply because they have a charter from the national government, rather than from a state government. Today, we do not have one central bank, but instead have twelve regional banks which were set up by the Federal Reserve Act of 1913.

Tariff. A tax on imported or foreign products. Some of the tariffs recommended by Hamilton were enacted in 1792. A tariff is designed to help local manufacturers by making the foreign product more expensive.

For example, the British made good quality, inexpensive woolen coats. Some Americans also went into this business, but with the price of constructing new factories and with high labor costs, they had to charge more than the British in order to make a profit. Consequently, the American consumer bought the cheaper British coat. But if a tax, or tariff, were added to the price of the British coat, then it became more expensive, and Americans bought their own product. In general, the tariff helped the manufacturer, but hurt the ordinary citizen who had to pay the higher price.

Excise tax. An internal tax on a product designed to raise money for the government. Hamilton encouraged Congress to pass excise taxes, such as one on whiskey, in order to finance the funding of the national debt and the assumption of state debts.

FOREIGN PROBLEMS

France.

1793, Citizen Genet Affair. In 1793 a general European war broke out and President Washington issued a proclamation of neutrality. The French sent a special representative, Edmond Charles Genet, to seek support from Americans anyway, by granting French military commissions and by licensing privateers to attack British shipping. Washington was annoyed at Genet's conduct and eventually asked that he be recalled to France. Meanwhile, however, his political associates had been overthrown in Paris, and rather than return to Europe, he sought political asylum and remained in the United States. He was referred to as "Citizen" Genet because in the French Revolution hereditary titles were abolished and people were simply referred to as "Citizen," much as the Russians today might use the word "Comrade."

England.

1795, Jay's Treaty. A treaty between the United States and England, signed in 1794 and ratified by the Senate in 1795. The American negotiator was John Jay and the treaty was unpopular and loudly criticized by the new Democratic-Republican Party. Included in the treaty:
--British evacuated posts along the Great Lakes.
--American shipowners compensated for seizures in the West Indies.
--American ships allowed to trade in the British East Indies, a term which refers to India and the adjacent area.

But:

--United States government must assure payment of pre-Revolutionary debts still owed British merchants.
--"Rule of 1756" recognized by Americans. It was a British regulation stating that neutral countries could not trade in wartime with ports that were normally closed to them in time of peace. In other words, simply because the British were distracted by a war with France, American ships could not move in and try to trade with Barbados, a British island in the Caribbean, which was closed to the United States, now that the United States was independent and no longer part of the British empire.
--"Most-favored nation" trade agreement granted to England. "Most-favored" is misleading, for in reality it means that no other country will get a better trade agreement although it may get equal treatment.

Spain.

1795, Pinckney's Treaty. Negotiated by Thomas Pinckney to settle disputes between United States and Spain. The treaty gave America full navigation rights to the Mississippi River and the right to deposit goods at New Orleans before sending them on ocean-going ships.

THE WEST

1795, Treaty of Greenville. Indians abandoned claims to much of the Northwest Territory. It followed the 1794 victory of General Anthony Wayne at the Battle of Fallen Timbers and the British refusal to continue supporting the Indians in that area.

1794, Whiskey Rebellion. Farmers in western Pennsylvania protested the excise tax on whiskey by interfering with the courts and terrorizing law enforcement officers.

President Washington considered their actions a threat to national authority, and called up 12,000 militiamen to break up the action. As a result of this show of force, the rebels ceased their activities and the tax was collected peaceably.

OTHER TERMS TO IDENTIFY

Adam Smith (1723-1790). A Scottish economist who published The Wealth of Nations in 1776. He opposed the closed trading systems advocated by mercantilism and favored free trade among nations. He opposed strict regulation of business by the government and instead supported non-intervention of government in the economic life of the country. His ideas greatly affected the United States' policies in the 19th and 20th centuries.

Charles Beard (1874-1948). An American historian who published an Economic Interpretation of the Constitution in 1913. His work suggested that the Founding Fathers at the Philadelphia Convention in 1787 were conservative, selfish businessmen trying to protect their own economic interests rather than being concerned with the needs of the majority. Much of Beard's controversial thesis has been discredited by more recent historians.

elastic clause. A clause in the Constitution which grants Congress the right to pass "all laws which shall be necessary and proper" to carry out their specified powers. This phrase can be used to stretch the Constitution and give Congress broad powers, or the word "necessary" can be interpreted literally and thus limit the powers of Congress.

GLOSSARY

bounty. A payment or reward given by the government for acts which will benefit the country. For example, during the colonial period royal bounties were paid to South Carolina indigo planters to encourage them to plant more indigo.

farthing. A British coin no longer used, which was worth one-fourth of a penny. The word is still used to mean a very small amount.

guillotine. Machine designed to behead persons by means of an ax or blade dropping down between two vertical posts. It was named after a French physician, J.I. Guillotin, who in 1789 proposed its use. This method of execution was commonly used during the French Revolution.

hard money. Gold and silver money, as opposed to paper. Today the term often refers to any stable currency.

Hercules. A hero in Greek mythology who possessed tremendous strength. While still a baby, two serpents were put into his cradle and he strangled them. Alexander Hamilton referred to the United States as a "Hercules in the cradle."

legal tender. Acceptable money, currency that may legally be offered in payment of a debt and that a creditor must accept.

powdered lackey. A uniformed or costumed male servant wearing a powdered wig. Washington tried to set a tone of formality by having powdered lackeys at the entry of his presidential mansion in New York.

staple product. A major item grown or produced in a region, such as tobacco in Virginia and fur in the Northwest Territory.

tonnage duty. A duty or charge per ton on cargo, which is usually paid at a port or on a canal. For example, the 1789 Tariff Act placed heavy tonnage duties on foreign shipping to encourage Americans to use United States' ships.

wampum. Small beads made from shells which were used by the Indians as currency.

DEFINE THE FOLLOWING, USING THE DICTIONARY IF NECESSARY

adjudicate
ameliorated
atypical
disparaged
ebullient
inextricably
intransigent
precipitous
sanguine
voraciously

SAMPLE QUESTIONS

MULTIPLE CHOICE

1. Delegates to the Annapolis Convention recommended the calling of another convention to:
   a. strengthen the state governments.
   b. write a new plan of government.
   c. revise the Articles of Confederation.
   d. none of the above.

2. The group which was the most outspoken against the new constitution (1787) was called:

a. Whig.
b. Federalist.
c. Antifederalist.
d. Loyalist.

3. The first capital under the new Constitutional government was:
   a. Boston.
   b. Washington, D.C.
   c. Philadelphia.
   d. New York City.

4. A tariff was proposed by Hamilton soon after the establishment of the government, partly to:
   a. prevent the flow of valuable raw materials to England.
   b. encourage American shipping.
   c. protect the wages of American labor.
   d. encourage American manufacturing.

5. Jay's Treaty with Great Britain:
   a. abrogated the Rule of 1756.
   b. discontinued payment of prewar debts.
   c. secured evacuation of northwest posts.
   d. settled issues of neutral rights.

TRUE-FALSE

1. The fact that under the Constitution, the President makes a treaty but the Senate must ratify it is an example of judicial review.

2. Stay laws benefited the debtor by delaying foreclosure on his property.

3. The assumption of state debts by the national government in exchange for locating the new capital in the South is an example of checks and balances.

4. In Pinckney's Treaty Spain granted full navigational rights to the Mississippi River and the right to deposit goods at New Orleans.

5. Citizen Genet encouraged the United States to remain neutral in the war between France and England.

ANSWERS
MULTIPLE CHOICE: c,c,d,c. TRUE-FALSE: F,T,F,T,F.

6

Jeffersonian Democracy

CHAPTER CHECKLIST

COMPARISON OF HAMILTON AND JEFFERSON

Hamilton.

--Helped form the Federalist party.
--Favored a strong central government.
--Represented the business-commercial interests.
--Favored England more than France.
--Advocated governmental control by the upper classes.
--Supported a national bank.
--Favored the theory of loose construction of the Constitution by invoking the elastic or "necessary and proper" clause.
--Received support in urban areas of the Northeast.

Jefferson.

--Helped found the Democratic-Republican party.
--Wanted a weak national government so as to conserve states'-rights.
--Represented the farming rather than the commercial interests.
--Favored France more than England.
--Felt government should be ruled by the informed masses.
--Encouraged state banks and was originally opposed to the national bank.
--Believed generally in a strict or literal interpretation of the Constitution.
--Received support in the agricultural South and Southwest.

DECLINE OF THE FEDERALISTS

1796, Washington's Farewell Address. Washington announced that he would not seek a third term, thus establishing a precedent which has only been broken by Franklin Roosevelt, who was elected four times. The speech is primarily remembered because he stated that Americans should avoid "permanent alliances," and later politicians used his argument to defend a policy of isolationism.

JOHN ADAMS (1735-1826), 2nd President

--Born in Massachusetts, graduated from Harvard, practiced law in Boston.
--Delegate at the First and Second Continental Congresses.
--Helped negotiate the 1783 Peace of Paris.
--First United States minister to England.
--Vice President under Washington.
--Member of the Federalist party.
--President (1797-1801).

<u>1797-1798, XYZ Affair</u>. A diplomatic controversy between the United States and France. Adams tried to end French interference with American shipping by sending three commissioners to Paris: Charles Pinckney, John Marshall, and Elbridge Gerry. They discovered that Talleyrand, the French foreign minister, expected a bribe of $250,000 before he would begin negotiations. The agents who asked for the bribes became known as X, Y, and Z, and their demand was refused by the Americans.

<u>1798, Alien and Sedition Acts</u>. A series of acts designed in part to hurt the Jeffersonian Republicans.

--Naturalization Act. A foreigner had to reside in the United States for 14 years rather than 5 years in order to be eligible for citizenship.
--Alien Enemies Act. President could arrest or expel citizens of a country with which the United States was at war.
--Alien Act. President could expel all aliens whom he considered dangerous.
--Sedition Act. Made it illegal to write or publish "false, scandalous, and malicious" writings against the United States government. Under its terms, twenty-five Republican newspaper editors and publishers were arrested for criticizing John Adams and his policies and ten were convicted.

<u>1798, Virginia and Kentucky Resolutions</u>. Passed by these two state legislatures in reaction to the Alien and Sedition Acts. The Virginia Resolution was written by James Madison and the Kentucky Resolution by Thomas Jefferson, and in theory they attempted to void the Alien and Sedition Acts within the borders of the two states. They presented the idea that a state, rather than the courts, could declare a law unconstitutional.

<u>Convention of 1800</u>. Abrogated, or officially abolished, the Franco-American treaties of 1778, under which the United States had supposedly been allies with France.

Election of 1800. According to the original Constitution each elector could vote for two men. The man with the majority of votes in the Electoral College would win, and his runner-up would be Vice President. If no one got a majority, the election would be decided in the House of Representatives with each state getting one vote. In the 1800 election the two Republicans, Thomas Jefferson and Aaron Burr, tied; the vote went to the House, and on the 36th ballot Jefferson became President by getting a majority of the states to vote for him.

1804, Twelfth Amendment. Provided for separate balloting in the Electoral College for President and Vice President, so that the runner-up would no longer be Vice President. This amendment was designed to prevent a recurrence of the problems in the 1800 election which had occurred because of the development of two well organized parties, a situation which the Founding Fathers had not foreseen.

Judiciary Act of 1801. Created six new circuit courts and sixteen new federal judges. Adams filled these positions with conservative Federalists. The new appointees were called "midnight justices" since rumor was that Adams had stayed up until midnight before Jefferson's inauguration to sign their commissions.

THOMAS JEFFERSON (1743-1826), 3rd President

- --Born in Virginia, attended the College of William and Mary, and practiced law.
- --Wrote the Declaration of Independence while a delegate to the Second Continental Congress.
- --Governor of Virginia.
- --Lived at Monticello, his estate in Virginia.
- --Diplomatic minister to France.
- --First Secretary of State.
- --Founded the Democratic-Republican party, along with James Madison.
- --Vice President under John Adams.
- --President (1801-1809).
- --Founder of the University of Virginia.
- --Died on July 4, 1826, the fiftieth anniversary of the Declaration, and the same day that John Adams died in Massachusetts.

JEFFERSON MET CHALLENGES

Judiciary.

1803, Marbury v. Madison. The first Supreme Court decision which declared part of a law unconstitutional. Before President Adams left office he had appointed William Marbury as a justice of the peace of the new District of Columbia. Although it had been signed, the commission had not been delivered, and Jefferson's secretary of state, James Madison, refused to do so. Marbury appealed to the Supreme Court to issue a writ of mandamus, that is, an order from the court ordering a public official to perform a specified duty, in this case to deliver the commission. Chief Justice John Marshall said Madison ought to deliver it but the Court had no power to make him do so because that part of the Judiciary Act of 1789 which granted the Supreme Court the power to issue a writ of mandamus had been unconstitutional.

Impeachment of judges. A majority vote in the House of Representatives is necessary to bring charges, or impeach, and a two-thirds vote of the members of the Senate present is required for conviction. Several Federalist judges were impeached. District Judge John Pickering was convicted and removed from the bench; Associate Justice of the Supreme Court Samuel Chase was acquitted.

Barbary States.

1801-1805, War with Tripoli. For decades North African Arab states demanded "protection" money from European and American ships. Jefferson tried to curtail the practice, and Tripoli declared war on the United States. Jefferson did not achieve his goal, for tribute payments continued until 1815. But a more favorable treaty was negotiated.

Louisiana.

--1682-1763. France
--1763-1800. Spain
--1800-1803. France
--1803- United States

1682, LaSalle. French explorer who reached the mouth of the Mississippi River and claimed all the land drained by the river and its tributaries for France, naming it after King Louis XIV.

1763, Treaty of Paris. Ended the Seven Years War and France gave Louisiana to Spain.

1800, Treaty of San Ildefonso. A secret treaty between Spain and France returning Louisiana to France, although the actual change did not take place until several years later. Napoleon wanted to grow food products in Louisiana to supply the French West Indian sugar islands, such as Santo Domingo.

1803, Louisiana Purchase. President Jefferson had sent James Monroe to join United States Senator Robert Livingston in Paris to attempt to purchase New Orleans and Florida. When Napoleon learned that he had lost the island of Santo Domingo he authorized his Foreign Minister Talleyrand to sell all of Louisiana to the United States. Livingston and Monroe exceeded their instructions and purchased the area for about $15 million.

New England Federalists.

1804, Essex Junto. A group of New England Federalists organized to break away from the Union and establish a "Northern Confederacy." They tried to get the support of Aaron Burr, who was running for governor of New York. When Burr lost, the scheme collapsed.

THE WEST

1804-1806, Lewis and Clark Expedition. Meriwether Lewis and William Clark led 48 men from St. Louis to the Pacific Ocean and back, gathering scientific data on plants, animals, and rocks, and establishing friendly relations with the Indians. Note the map "Exploring the Louisiana Purchase" on p. 166.

OTHER TERMS TO IDENTIFY

Democratic-Republican Party. Founded by James Madison and Thomas Jefferson in the mid 1790's. It was generally referred to as the Republican Party. In the 1820's, Andrew Jackson changed the name of the party to Democratic. The Jeffersonian Republican party is today's Democratic party. The present Republican party started in the 1850's.

Citizen Pierre Adet. A French minister to the United States who tried to block ratification of the 1795 Jay Treaty with England and campaigned against the pro-British John Adams in the 1796 presidential elections.

John Marshall (1755-1835). A Virginian who became a leader in the Federalist Party. During Adams' administration he served as minister to France, a member of the House of Representatives, and as secretary of state. Adams appointed Marshall to the Supreme Court where he served as Chief Justice from 1801-1835.

Stephen Decatur (1779-1820). A naval officer who won fame in the war with Tripoli and later in the War of 1812 against England.

Napoleon Bonaparte (1769-1821). A military officer who became commander of the French army in 1795, head of the government in 1799, and who crowned himself emperor in 1804. After trying to conquer much of Europe and North Africa he was finally defeated at the Battle of Waterloo in 1815.

Santo Domingo. Today the island of Hispaniola in the Caribbean is shared by two countries: the Spanish-speaking Dominican Republic and Haiti where a French-Spanish-

African mixture called French creole is spoken. The capital city of the present day Dominican Republic is called Santo Domingo, although formerly the whole island went by that name.

--1492. Columbus claimed Santo Domingo for Spain.

--1697. France received western one-third of island.

--1791. Racial unrest and revolt broke out on the French side led by Toussaint L'Ouverture, a former slave.

--1795. Spain ceded her portion of the island to France, but regained it in 1814.

--1802. General Leclerc and French soldiers tried to recapture the island but failed, primarily because of yellow fever.

--1804. The French colony became independent and was named Haiti.

--1821. Santo Domingo became independent from Spain.

Sacagawea. A Shoshoni squaw who, along with her French-Canadian husband, served as guide for the Lewis and Clark expedition.

Zebulon Pike (1779-1813). An army officer and explorer who made expeditions into the Louisiana territory and the Spanish southwest. He discovered the Colorado peak named for him. See the map "Exploring the Louisiana Purchase" on p. 166.

GLOSSARY

Continental Divide. A long stretch of high ground from each side of which the river systems of a continent flow in opposite directions. In North America the Continental Divide is formed by the crests of the Rocky Mountains.

Francophile. Someone who is pro-French or a lover of French things. Jefferson was considered a Francophile.

Gallic. A term which means French, such as Gallic food. It is from the word Gaul, the ancient name for the territory which now includes France and Belgium.

Junto. A small, usually secret group that gathers for some common aim or purpose. The Essex Junto met to discuss secession of the New England states from the United States.

liberté, égalité, fraternité. A French phrase meaning liberty, equality, brotherhood. It was used in France to describe the goals of the French Revolution and has since been used in other areas of the world to symbolize democratic movements.

pirogue. A canoe made from a hollowed tree trunk. Lewis and Clark used pirogues as they pushed up the Mississippi River in 1804. Today pirogues are still used in the bayous of Louisiana.

quasi-war. An undeclared conflict which resembles a war. The United States was involved in a quasi-war with France in the late 1790's.

Spartan. A person who resembles the Spartans in their indifference to physical discomforts, their austere manner of living, and their self-discipline. Sparta was an area in Greece where civilization flourished from the 7th to the 4th centuries B.C. Jefferson was considered somewhat of a Spartan in that he did not smoke, drink, hunt, or gamble.

DEFINE THE FOLLOWING, USING THE DICTIONARY IF NECESSARY

acrimonious
anathemas
canard
dichotomy
dumbwaiter
juggernaut
laconic
metaphysical
pasha
pusillanimity
querulous

SAMPLE QUESTIONS

MULTIPLE CHOICE

1. In his Farewell Address, George Washington:
   a. encouraged the growth of political parties.
   b. warned against forming permanent alliances.
   c. encouraged the country to seek better relations with England.
   d. abrogated the treaty with Spain.

2. All of the following are accomplishments of Thomas Jefferson except:
   a. founder of the University of Virginia.
   b. member of the Constitutional Convention.
   c. principal author of the Declaration of Independence.
   d. Vice President for one term and President for two terms.

3. According to the Virginia and Kentucky Resolutions, where did the right to determine the constitutionality of an act of Congress finally reside?
   a. in Congress.
   b. in the states.
   c. in the President.
   d. in the Supreme Court.

4. Flags flew over Louisiana in which of the following chronological orders?
   a. France, Spain, United States.
   b. Spain, Mexico, France, United States.

   c. Spain, France, Spain, United States.
   d. France, Spain, France, United States.

5. In taking a position on the creation of the Bank of the United States, Thomas Jefferson expressed one point of view concerning his interpretation of the Constitution. In purchasing Louisiana he took another. Which one of the following represents Jefferson's position in regard to the purchase of Louisiana?
   a. laissez faire.
   b. isolationism.
   c. strict constructionist.
   d. loose constructionist.

TRUE-FALSE

1. Alexander Hamilton was considered a Francophile.

2. The 12th Amendment to the Constitution provided for a new method to elect the Vice President in the Electoral College.

3. Impeachment is the process of jailing people for criticizing the government.

4. <u>Marbury v. Madison</u> is the first example of judicial review by the Supreme Court.

5. James Madison was one of the founders of the Democratic-Republican party.

<u>ANSWERS</u>
MULTIPLE CHOICE: b,b,b,d,d. TRUE-FALSE: F,T,F,T,T.

7
America Escapes from Europe

CHAPTER CHECKLIST

TROUBLEMAKERS FOR JEFFERSON

John Randolph of Roanoke. A member of the House of Representatives from Virginia for nearly 30 years. He generally took a strong states'-rights position, and from 1804 he opposed Jefferson and his programs. Note the picture of Randolph on p. 172.

Quids. The conservative, states'-rights faction within the Republican party, led by John Randolph.

Yazoo land frauds. A land scandal in Georgia named from the Yazoo River running through part of the area in question. In 1795 the Georgia legislature sold territory in what is now Alabama and Mississippi to four land companies. When it was learned that the companies had bribed the legislators the grant was rescinded, or cancelled, even though some of the land had already been sold. Those who had bought land denied Georgia's right to rescind the law and sought a remedy from Congress. Finally, Congress voted money to be granted to the victims of the Yazoo frauds. In 1810 the Supreme Court decision Fletcher v. Peck declared that Georgia's rescinding law had been unconstitutional.

1806-1807, Burr Conspiracy. Aaron Burr became involved in a western land scheme which led to his being tried for treason and acquitted. Whether he planned to detach part of western United States or conquer a section of the Spanish southwest is still unclear. However, his actions were betrayed by Louisiana territorial governor James Wilkinson and Burr was brought to Virginia for trial. John Marshall presided at the trial, not as Chief Justice but as a member of the circuit court. Marshall encouraged a narrow definition of treason, and Burr was acquitted.

COMMERCIAL WARFARE WITH ENGLAND AND FRANCE

1799-1815, Napoleonic Wars. A series of wars in Europe with England and France on opposite sides. One method of fighting was to disrupt each other's economy through blocking trade. This tactic greatly affected Americans, who were trading with both sides.

1806, Berlin Decree. Issued by France, stating that all commerce with Great Britain was illegal.

1807, British Orders in Council. Instructions that ships could not go to ports on the European continent unless they first stopped at a British port and paid customs duties.

1807, Milan Decree. The French declared that any ship which stopped at a British port and paid duties would then be subject to seizure by the French.

Continental System. Napoleon's scheme of economic warfare against the British. He wanted to keep English ships out of ports on the European continent.

Impressment. The British practice of forcibly drafting Englishmen for service in the Royal Navy in emergencies. There were several methods of impressing sailors. One was to send "press gangs" into pubs in British ports. Another was to stop British merchant ships at sea and go aboard to impress sailors. A third was to stop neutral ships to look for British citizens. It was the third metho which angered Americans because not only were British impressed but also Americans.

June, 1807: Leopard - Chesapeake incident. The British frigate Leopard hailed the American frigate Chesapeake and demanded that the British be allowed on board to search for four deserters. When the American commander refused, the Leopard fired on the American ship, the Chesapeake was forced to surrender, and the alleged deserters were seized. This action angered the American public and many wanted war.

December, 1807-March, 1809: Embargo Act. An act which forbade all exports from the United States. Jefferson hoped to prevent future Leopard-Chesapeake incidents, and he also hoped the boycott would put economic pressure on the European powers. The Embargo was unpopular among American merchants and was violated to some extent. However, it did mean a sharp decline in exports. Note the text chart "American Foreign Trade, 1790-1812" on p. 178.

1809, Non-Intercourse Act. A United States law which forbade trade with Great Britain and France. If either country stopped violating American rights, the United States would resume trade with that country.

1810, Macon's Bill No. 2. A law named after Representative Nathaniel Macon which stated that the United States would trade with both France and Great Britain. But if either country stopped violating American rights, we would cease trade with the other. Soon after, Napoleon tricked Madison into believing that France would change her actions, so the United States stopped trading with Great Britain.

JAMES MADISON (1751-1836), 4th President

--Born in Virginia, graduated from the College of New Jersey (Princeton).
--Delegate at the Continental Congress.
--Delegate at the Constitutional Convention, where he argued for a strong central government.
--Worked for ratification of the Constitution by writing some of The Federalist Papers.
--A founder of the Democratic-Republican Party.
--Wrote the Virginia Resolution opposing the Alien and Sedition Acts.
--Secretary of State under Jefferson.
--President (1809-1817).

OTHER PROBLEMS LEADING TO WAR

Indians. They wanted to keep their lands.

--Tecumseh (1768-1813). A Shawnee chief who bound together the tribes east of the Mississippi in a confederation. Its purpose was to stop the advance of the white man into the Ohio Valley. During the War of 1812 Tecumseh fought alongside the British against the Americans and was killed in battle. Note the picture of Tecumseh on p. 181.
--The Prophet. Brother of Tecumseh and a medicine man. He led a religious and cultural revival while Tecumseh built a political and military confederation.
--1811, Battle of Tippecanoe. Fought between Indians led by the Prophet and American troops led by General William Henry Harrison, governor of the Indiana Territory. The Indians attacked Harrison's camp, fell back, and then Harrison's troops destroyed Prophetstown, the village which the Indians had founded in 1808, where Tippecanoe Creek joins the Wabash River. The battle is significant because it shattered Tecumseh's Indian confederation, made Harrison a national hero, and convinced many western settlers, incorrectly, that the British had incited the Indians.

Depression and Land Hunger. The slow transportation and distribution system plus American commercial restrictions contributed to falling agricultural prices. At the same time, farmers wanted more land in the West.

War Hawks. The name given to young Democratic-Republican congressmen who from 1810 to 1812 urged the United States to protect its national honor and fight the British. They were concerned about impressment and commercial warfare, but they also wanted to stop the Indian problems in the West and to acquire Canada.

THE WAR OF 1812

1812-1814. Great Britain devoted little attention to the war in the United States. She was preoccupied in war with Napoleon's French troops, who were defeated at the 1815 Battle of Waterloo.

1814, Burning of Washington, D.C.. When defenses fell at nearby Bladensburg, President Madison and government officials fled the capital. British troops burned many of the public buildings, including the White House. This action marked a low point for the Americans in the war.

1814, "The Star-Spangled Banner." After burning Washington, the British troops sailed toward Baltimore, Maryland, which was guarded by Fort McHenry. Francis Scott Key, a Maryland attorney, came on board one of the British ships to secure the release of an American prisoner. He was detained when the bombardment started, and through the night he watched to see if the American flag was still flying over Fort McHenry. The next morning he wrote the words to "The Star-Spangled Banner" which was later set to the tune of a popular English song "To Anacreon in Heaven." It was officially adopted as the national anthem in 1913.

1815, Treaty of Ghent. Signed in Ghent, Belgium, on December 24, 1814, and ratified by the Senate in 1815, this treaty ended the War of 1812. It was essentially an agreement to stop fighting since neither side made concessions. The British and the Americans agreed to restore all conquered territory and return to the status quo ante bellum, that is, just as things were before the war.

1814-1815, Hartford Convention. A gathering of New England Federalists in Hartford, Connecticut, to protest the War of 1812 and to propose amendments to the Constitution. It was the New England commercial interests who were hardest hit by the Embargo and by the wartime blockade. A few proposed separation from the Union. When news of the Treaty of Ghent arrived, their plans were ignored, and their party discredited. The Hartford Convention is sometimes considered the "dying gasp" of the Federalist Party.

1815, Battle of New Orleans. A great victory for the Americans, led by General Andrew Jackson, which took place after the treaty had been signed. After two weeks of probing the American line five miles below New Orleans, the British General Pakenham ordered an assault on January 8. When the bugles finally signaled retreat, the British had suffered 2,100 casualties, and another 500 were prisoners; eight Americans died, and thirteen were wounded. The battle strengthened American pride and nationalism, and made Andrew Jackson a national hero.

RESULTS OF THE WAR

Feelings of nationalism were increased. People felt pride in being Americans. European nations viewed the United States with new respect, realizing that our republican form of government was not going to be just a temporary experiment.

Indians were pushed farther west. As a result, new lands were opened to settlers.

Federalist Party was destroyed. The party had experienced a brief revival led by a group known as the Young Federalists. But when the war which they opposed ended, their views found no support. The party ran its last presidential candidate, Rufus King, in the election of 1816.

Relations with England improved.

--1817, Rush-Bagot Agreement. Began the demilitarization of the United States-Canadian border. This agreement limited armed vessels on the Great Lakes to each power having one 100-ton vessel armed with an 18-pounder on Lake Champlain and another on Lake Ontario. An 18-pounder was a cannon, mounted on a ship, which fired cannon balls weighing 18 pounds.
--Convention of 1818. Allowed for the joint control of the Oregon territory for 10 years after which the agreement could be renewed. In addition it set the 49th parallel as the northern boundary of the Louisiana Territory between the Lake of the Woods and the Rocky Mountains. Note the map entitled "The United States 1819" on p. 194.

EXPANDING UNITED STATES' ROLE IN THE CONTINENT

1819, Transcontinental Treaty. Negotiated by Secretary of State John Quincy Adams and Spanish minister in Washington, Luis de Onís, and ratified by the Senate in 1821. The United States acquired Florida in exchange for assuming $5 million in claims which the Spanish government owed American citizens. The treaty also established the Spanish boundary from Louisiana to the Pacific Ocean. Spain abandoned her claims to the territory north of California, and the United States abandoned claims to Texas. See the map "The United States 1819" on p. 194.

Florida.

--1513. Claimed by Ponce de Leon for Spain.

--1763-1783. Owned by England, then returned to Spain.
--1813. United States troops seized West Florida.
--1818. General Jackson raided Seminole settlements in Florida.
--1819. Adams-Onís Transcontinental Treaty signed.
--1821. Senate ratified the treaty, and Florida became part of the United States.

1823, Monroe Doctrine. A statement of foreign policy which proclaimed that the United States would not meddle in European affairs and Europe should not interfere in the United States or in other countries in this hemisphere. These ideas, formulated by Secretary of State Adams and Monroe, were presented in President Monroe's annual message on December 2, 1823. The message was in response to two problems -- Russian claims to the Northwest Coast and the independence of Latin America. It stated:
--North and South America were no longer open to European colonization. This portion was to discourage the Russians on the Pacific.
--The United States would not bother colonies which belonged to European powers, such as Canada, Puerto Rico, or Martinique.
--Europe's political system was different from that developing in this hemisphere and the two should not be mixed. The Latin American countries which had won their independence by 1821 had set up republics rather than monarchies, with the exception of Brazil which had an emperor until 1889.
--This policy statement was simply a speech, not international law, and had no real meaning until years later when the United States had the power to enforce it. It is still used today when the United States feels a European country is overly interfering in the affairs of a country in this hemisphere; a recent example is the 1962 protest to Russia when she attempted to establish missile bases in Cuba.

OTHER TERMS TO IDENTIFY

Albert Gallatin (1761-1849). Secretary of the Treasury under Presidents Jefferson and Madison. Although a Jeffersonian Republican, his financial policies did not sharply differ from those of the original Treasury Secretary Hamilton. Gallatin was a negotiator at the Treaty of Ghent and later United States minister to France and to Great Britain. He was also interested in Indian languages and customs and in 1842 founded the American Ethnological Society.

James Wilkinson (1757-1825). A professional soldier who at intervals in his career was suspected of accepting bribes. He was in the pay of the Spanish when as governor of Louisiana territory in 1805-1806 he discussed with Aaron

Burr various aspects of Burr's western schemes. Then Wilkinson betrayed Burr's activities to President Jefferson and was the prosecution's chief witness at the trial.

Rule of War of 1756. The British denied to neutrals the right to engage in trade during time of war from which they were banned by mercantilistic regulations in time of peace. For example, sugar from the French island of Martinique was to be carried to France in French ships. But during the Napoleonic Wars French ships were bottled up in port or distracted elsewhere so United States ships tried to appropriate this trade. The British applied the Rule of 1756 and captured the American ships.

Re-export trade. As a way of getting around the Rule of 1756, Americans brought products from the West Indies to the United Atates first, and then reshipped them to Europe, claiming that since the products had touched American soil they were now American products.

GLOSSARY

Attila. A king of the Germanic tribe called the Huns from 434 to 453 A.D., he led a bloodthirsty invasion of Europe. Jefferson once referred to Napoleon Bonaparte as "the Attila of the age."

bayou. A marshy body of water which is a tributary to a lake or river. The term, based on an Indian word, was originally used by the French in Louisiana.

claims. Demands for payment made by the citizens of one country to the government of another. For example, if Indians from Spanish Florida raided Georgia and burned down a barn, then the owner might file a claim with the Spanish government demanding payment for the lost property. In the 1819 Transcontinental Treaty the United States government assumed $5 million in claims which American citizens had been demanding from the Spanish government.

dog-in-the-manger attitude. An allusion to the fable of the dog that stationed himself in the manger and would not let the ox or horse eat the hay. The dog did not want the hay, but he did not want the other animals to have it either. The Federalists had a dog-in-the-manger attitude toward the War of 1812.

frigate. A high-speed, medium-sized sailing vessel used from the 17th through the 19th centuries.

palindrome. A word or phrase which reads the same forward or backward. During Jefferson's embargo a cartoonist created an imaginary specie of snapping turtle which he called the "ograbme," the palindrome of embargo. Note the cartoon on p. 178.

<u>paper blockade</u>. An attempt to cut off trade to a port or area by passing governmental decrees which state that order. France tried to establish a paper blockade with England through the Berlin and Milan Decrees, but she did not have the naval power to enforce it effectively.

<u>parapet</u>. An earthen or stony embankment protecting soldiers from enemy fire. At the Battle of New Orleans Jackson's troops erected an earthen parapet about ten yards behind a dry creek bed, and there they made their stand against the British.

<u>rapprochement</u>. A re-establishment of cordial relations, as between two countries. After the War of 1812 an Anglo-American rapprochement emerged, that is, relations between the two countries improved.

<u>state's evidence</u>. Evidence voluntarily given by an accomplice who confesses the crime and testifies in court against his previous associates. President Jefferson ordered blanket pardons to co-conspirators of Aaron Burr who would agree to turn state's evidence.

<u>treason</u>. The offense of attempting by overt acts to overthrow the government of one's own country. Treason in the United States is defined in the Constitution (Article III, Section 3) as consisting "only in levying War against them, or in adhering to their Enemies, giving them Aid and Comfort. No Person shall be convicted of Treason unless on the Testimony of two Witnesses to the same Overt Act, or on Confession in open Court." Aaron Burr was tried for treason, but not convicted.

<u>"twisting the British lion's tail."</u> A term used in the 19th century referring to the Americans' practice of criticizing policies and making jokes at the expense of Great Britain. The lion is the symbol of England.

<u>DEFINE THE FOLLOWING, USING THE DICTIONARY IF NECESSARY</u>

amphibious
anomalous
epigram
immutable
largess
macabre
obtuse
parsimonious
pithy
psychosomatic

SAMPLE QUESTIONS

MULTIPLE CHOICE

1. Aaron Burr was involved with each of these except:
   a. the "Northern Confederacy" in 1804.
   b. General James Wilkinson in the West.
   c. the Yazoo land frauds.
   d. a treason trial.

2. The order "No ship shall clear from the United States for any foreign port. No ship shall depart even for another American port without giving bond...that the goods will be relanded within the United States" is part of the:
   a. Berlin Decree.
   b. Embargo Act.
   c. Non-intervention Act.
   d. Macon's Bill No. 2.

3. Which of the following was a factor in the American decision to declare war on Great Britain in 1812?
   a. British Orders in Council.
   b. conflict between the British and Americans on the frontier.
   c. impressment.
   d. all of these.

4. The Hartford Convention was attended by:
   a. Federalists.
   b. Republicans.
   c. War Hawks.
   d. Jacksonians.

5. The Battle of New Orleans in 1815 was:
   a. a costly British victory.
   b. fought after the signing of the peace.
   c. a costly American victory.
   d. a feather in the cap of General Harrison.

TRUE-FALSE

1. John Randolph and the Quids were strong supporters of President Jefferson.

2. "Once an Englishman, always an Englishman" was an argument used by the British in support of the practice of impressment.

3. The Rush-Bagot Treaty began the demilitarization of the United States-Canadian border.

4. In the Transcontinental Treaty, the United States received the Oregon territory in return for paying American citizens $5 million in claims.

5. "The American continents...are not to be considered as subjects for future colonization" was a portion of the 1823 Monroe Doctrine.

ANSWERS
<u>MULTIPLE</u> CHOICE: c,b,d,a,b. TRUE-FALSE: F,T,T,F,T.

8

New Forces in American Life

CHAPTER CHECKLIST

> JAMES MONROE (1758-1831), 5th President
>
> --Born in Virginia, studied law with Thomas Jefferson.
> --United States Senator from Virginia.
> --Minister to France under Washington.
> --Governor of Virginia.
> --Helped negotiate the Louisiana Purchase.
> --Secretary of State and then Secretary of War under Monroe.
> --President (1817-1825).
> --"Era of Good Feelings" was term used to describe his presidency.
> --Last of the "Virginia dynasty" presidents.

NEW ELEMENTS IN THE ECONOMY

Factory system. Effectively introduced by Samuel Slater in making cotton thread.

Assembly line system of production. Made possible by Eli Whitney's precise methods of manufacturing parts for rifles which made the parts interchangeable.

Automation. Used by Oliver Evans in flour milling, for example. One man poured grain down the chute, the other headed, that is, put the top on, the barrel of flour. All intervening steps of weighing, cleaning, grinding, and packing were performed by machines.

Regularly scheduled steamboats. John Fitch first operated steamboats on the Mississippi in 1790. They helped bring the West into the national economy.

Cotton gin. Invention by Eli Whitney designed to separate seeds from the fiber; made possible large-scale cotton cultivation in the South and caused a revival of slavery.

Bank of the United States. Existed from 1791 to 1811 and from 1816 to 1836, and was an important source of credit for business transactions.

Corporation. A company chartered by the states with certain rights and duties. At this time only companies with semi-public "products," such as roads, canals, insurance companies, and waterworks were incorporated.

THE FACTORY

Samuel Slater (1768-1835). He is credited with the first effective introduction of the factory system into the United States. He set up machines to make cotton thread in Pawtucket, Rhode Island, in 1790. Slater was a textile mechanic in England, and the British, in order to protect their textile industry, barred both the export of textile machinery and the emigration of textile workers. Slater, however, memorized the plans for the machines and secretly emigrated to the United States where the Quaker merchant Moses Brown financed his construction of a cotton spinning mill.

Francis Cabot Lowell (1775-1817). He designed an efficient power loom and set up the Boston Manufacturing Company at Waltham, Massachusetts. Lowell headed a group of merchants called the Boston Associates who between 1813 and 1850 built a number of large factories that revolutionized textile production. They concentrated upon the mass production of a standardized product: cheap, durable cloth.

"Lowell System." The efficient system used by Lowell and the Boston Associates in manufacturing cloth. It combined machine production, large-scale operation, professional management, and centralized marketing. Even though its efficiency was obvious, most manufacturing in the first half of the 1800's was still done by local craftsmen and traveling artisans.

LABOR

Craftsman. A worker in the trades started out as an apprentice to a master for a period of five to seven years. Then he became a journeyman, working for wages. Finally, he could become a master craftsman and set up a shop of his own. His importance began to decline as a cheap, efficient product became more sought after than a finely finished one.

Factory workers. Women and children took many of the factory positions because machines lessened the need for both skill and strength.

--"Waltham System". A system developed by the Boston Associates of employing unmarried girls and housing them in company dormitories. It was named after their Waltham, Massachusetts, textile company.

Slaves. The importance of slavery was revived by the increased production of cotton made possible by the cotton gin. See the charts "Cotton Production, 1800-1860" and "Slave Population, 1800-1860," on p. 211.

--Increased need for slaves. While visiting a plantation near Savannah, Georgia, in 1793, Eli Whitney invented the cotton gin which revolutionized the cotton business. With a machine which could separate the seeds from the lint it became profitable to grow greenseed, or upland, cotton, and thus more slaves were needed to work the expanding cotton fields.
--Importation of slaves. The Constitution prohibited the importation of slaves from outside the United States after 1808.
--Interstate traffic in slaves. The importation of slaves into a state in order to sell them was prohibited by some states in the late 18th century. These laws were increasingly evaded and by 1820 some states were changing their laws to permit interstate slave trade.

Free blacks.

--American Colonization Society. Founded in 1817 by whites to send free blacks to Africa if they wished to go. The society purchased land in Africa and established the Republic of Liberia. Only about 12,000 Negroes emigrated and the society's efforts declined rapidly after 1830.
--Negroes in northern states. Free blacks were generally denied civil rights such as voting or testifying in court. They could not get decent jobs or housing, and they faced discrimination in hospitals, churches, restaurants, and public transportation.

TRANSPORTATION

Roads. A network of roads was needed for trade to move from the Mississippi Valley to the eastern seaboard. Building decent roads across the Appalachian Mountains was difficult. Steep grades had to be reduced, drainage ditches were essential, and a firm foundation of stones topped with gravel was necessary.

Bridges. These were improved in design and construction. Stone bridges and wooden truss bridges were used. A truss was a framework of wooden beams, often arranged in triangles, to support a bridge.

Turnpikes. Roads, built either by private companies or by states, which charged a fee or toll for using them.

Internal improvements. The general term used in the early 1800's to refer to the upgrading of transportation facilities, such as roads and canals. Some felt it was unconstitutional for the national government to become involved in these projects.

Water. The cheapest form of transportation.

--Steamboat. In 1807 on the Hudson River Robert Fulton launched the Clermont, the first successful commercial steamboat. He was financed by Robert Livingston and for a while they held a monopoly on steamboat trade in New York waters and on the lower Mississippi River. The steamboat made freight charges decline sharply. In addition it was a comfortable way for passengers to travel.

--Canal. This form of artificial waterway was expensive to build but made a cheap form of transportation. Goods were placed on barges drawn by horses walking on towpaths along the banks of the canal. The Erie Canal was built in 1817-1825 to link the Hudson River with the Great Lakes, and indirectly New York City with the Midwest. Its construction was encouraged by DeWitt Clinton, and it cost over 7 million dollars. It opened up trade to the Midwest, it cemented New York City's position as the nation's leading port, and the success of the Erie sparked a nationwide canal-building boom. Note the map "Canals and Roads 1820-1850" on pp. 222-223.

GOVERNMENT AND BUSINESS

Corporation laws. Passed by several states, including Massachusetts and New York. In most cases separate authorizations for each charter were given by the state legislatures, rather than having general incorporation laws.

Tax benefits. Manufacturers in some states received tax breaks. For example, a New York law of 1817 exempted mills from taxation.

Patent office. Created in 1790 to protect inventors. If a person tried to pirate a registered patent, he was subject to prosecution by the law.

SUPREME COURT DECISIONS

John Marshall. Chief Justice from 1801 to 1835. His decisions reflected his belief in a strong central government and a national view of economic affairs. Between 1819 and 1824 the Court handed down a number of decisions which affected the business community and the government.

1819, Sturges v. Crowninshield. Upheld the importance of contracts. This decision declared a New York bankruptcy law unconstitutional because the state had applied the law to debts incurred before the law was passed. Debts were considered contracts.

1819, Dartmouth College v. Woodward. Stated that a charter granted by the state was a contract and could not be altered or cancelled without the consent of both parties. The state of New Hampshire tried to change Dartmouth from a private to a public institution but the Supreme Court said that it could not alter the charter granted to the college by the king in 1769.

1819, McCulloch v. Maryland. Asserted the supremacy of the federal government over the state governments. The state of Maryland had placed a tax on the bank notes of all banks not chartered by the state. This law was designed to tax the second Bank of the United States, which had a branch in Baltimore. In this decision, Chief Justice Marshall justified the constitutionality of the Bank and indicated that the state could not tax it.

1824, Gibbons v. Ogden. A decision which consolidated national power over commerce by regulating interstate trade. The decision destroyed the steamboat monopoly on the Hudson River held by Aaron Ogden. It proclaimed that a state could regulate trade within its own borders but when part of a river's banks were shared with another state, in this case New Jersey, then the national government or court had jurisdiction, and the Supreme Court ruled against this monopoly.

OTHER TERMS TO IDENTIFY

Era of Good Feelings. A phrase used to describe the period from 1817 to 1825 when James Monroe was president. There was only one political party at this time, the Democratic-Republican, and Monroe tried to woo formerly Federalist New England by making a good-will tour early in his administration. Monroe was greeted enthusiastically, and a Federalist newspaperman remarked on this new political unity by calling the times the "Era of Good Feelings." This phrase is not entirely accurate, however, for it was also a time of sectional and personal controversy.

Liberia. A country whose name means "place of freedom," founded on the west coast of Africa by the American Colonization Society. The purpose of the Society was to encourage slaveholders to free their slaves, and in 1820 it sent 88 blacks along with several white associates to this area in Africa which the members had purchased. In 1822 the settlers founded Monrovia, named after the United States president, which is today the capital of the country. In 1847 the colony broke its ties with the American Colonization Society and set up an independent republic, with a government modelled on that of the United States. Today in Liberia the ruling class is largely composed of the descendants of the freed slaves who colonized the area, while much of the population still follows its traditional tribal way of life.

Old National Road. Constructed by the national government from 1811 to 1818 and ran from Cumberland, Maryland, to Wheeling, in what is now West Virginia. It was gradually extended as far west as Vandalia, Illinois, by 1852. Note the map "Canals and Roads 1820-1850." Although some felt that even major interstate arteries should be financed by states and not by the federal government, this project continued and became the most important east-west land route between the Ohio Valley and the East.

Robert Fulton (1765-1815). Artist, engineer, inventor who spent twenty years in Europe, principally London and Paris, where he studied painting and invented a number of mechanical devices. His inventions included a power shovel for digging canals, a rope twister, designs for cast-iron bridges, a submarine, and a self-propelled submarine torpedo. His most famous design was the Clermont, the first successful commercial steamboat.

DeWitt Clinton (1769-1828). A reform minded politician who was mayor of New York City from 1803 to 1815 and governor of the state from 1817 to 1821 and from 1825 to 1828. He fought for free public education, education of women, and aid for minorities such as blacks and Indians. He is most famous for sponsoring the Erie Canal, which some of his opponents called "Clinton's Big Ditch."

GLOSSARY

Archimedes screw. A device which looks like a long screw. By turning it, an object such as flour or water is moved along from one point to another. It is named after the Greek inventor and mathematician, Archimedes (287-212 B.C.). In Oliver Evans' automated gristmill pictured on p. 201, the grain moved vertically by bucket and horizontally by Archimedes screw.

brogan. A heavy, ankle-high work shoe. The growing shoe industry in the early 1800's concentrated on producing rough brogans for slaves and western farmers, rather than on making finely crafted shoes which required more skill.

Conestoga wagon. A heavy covered wagon with broad wheels, used by American pioneers for westward travel. The wagons were first built at Conestoga, Pennsylvania.

delta. The area near the mouth of a river where soil deposits are left by the wash of the river. It is usually triangular in shape, and thus derives its name from delta, the fourth letter of the Greek alphabet, which is the shape of a triangle. After the War of 1812 the delta region along the lower Mississippi River became important as a cotton raising area.

manumission. The act of freeing slaves.

mulatto. A person of mixed white and black ancestry.

prima facie. A Latin phrase which literally means "on first appearance." It can also be interpreted as "at first sight" or "before closer inspection."

spinning jenny. An early form of spinning machine which had several spindles. A spindle is a rod which holds the spool of thread.

truck-garden. A farm which produces vegetables for market. This type of commercial agriculture flourished around manufacturing centers which needed food, as many agricultural workers left the farms and sought jobs in industry.

DEFINE THE FOLLOWING, USING THE DICTIONARY IF NECESSARY

emporium
idyll
inviolable
libertarian
paradoxically
photostatic
trousseau
ubiquitous

SAMPLE QUESTIONS

MULTIPLE CHOICE

1. The "Era of Good Feelings" witnessed the disappearance of which one of the following political parties?
   a. The Republican party.
   b. The Democratic-Republican party.
   c. The Federalist party.
   d. The Whig party.

2. A system developed by the Boston Associates of employing unmarried girls and housing them in company dormitories was called the:
   a. Lowell System.
   b. Waltham System.
   c. closed shop.
   d. apprentice system.

3. Which of the following pairs is incorrect?
   a. Eli Whitney: cotton gin.
   b. Samuel Slater: steamboat.
   c. Francis Cabot Lowell: power loom.

d. Oliver Evans: flour-milling machine.

4. The purpose of the American Colonization Society was:
   a. to settle Americans west of the Appalachian Mountains.
   b. to bring over Irish to help build the Erie Canal.
   c. to send freed slaves to Africa.
   d. to remove Indians from Spanish Florida.

5. The principal trend in Supreme Court decisions while John Marshall was Chief Justice was:
   a. to weaken the position of the federal courts in the national government.
   b. to expand the powers of the national government.
   c. to strengthen the power of the states at the expense of the national government.
   d. to make the western states subordinate to those of the East.

TRUE-FALSE

1. The Constitution prohibited the importation of slaves from 1808.

2. Election and political reforms were known as internal improvements.

3. The Erie Canal was designed to link the Great Lakes with the Hudson River.

4. Textile factory workers were mainly adult males because the machines required their skills and physical strength.

5. McCulloch v. Maryland asserted the supremacy of the federal government over the state government of Maryland.

ANSWERS
MULTIPLE CHOICE: c,b,b,c,b. TRUE-FALSE: T,F,T,F,T.

9

The Emergence of Sectionalism

CHAPTER CHECKLIST

SECTIONS OF THE COUNTRY

Northeast. The area north and east of Maryland was bound by a common concern with manufacturing.

South. There was a common bond of slavery and the agricultural staples, especially cotton.

West. The region between the Appalachian Mountains and the Mississippi River was a varied, changing zone which was not as cohesive politically as the other two sections.

SECTIONAL POLITICAL ISSUES OF THE 1820'S

Tariff. A tax on imports designed to protect domestic industries from foreign competition. The manufacturing North favored high protective tariffs, although New England shipping interests preferred free trade. Southerners rejected protection. It not only made their purchases higher at home, but they feared other countries would retaliate by placing tariffs on products such as cotton and tobacco which the South needed to sell to them.

National banking policy. The second Bank of the United States was authorized in 1816 with a 20-year charter. Sectional lines were not sharply drawn on this issue. More Northern congressmen voted against the new Bank than for it, Southern congressmen supported it, as did Westerners , although the West opposed the Bank after the Panic of 1819.

Land policy. The West wanted public land to be sold cheaply. The North and South felt the government should get as much cash from it as possible. Northern manufacturers feared cheap western land would drain off surplus labor and force rates up. Southern planters were concerned about competition which would develop from cotton being grown in the Southwest.

NORTHERN LEADERS

Daniel Webster (1782-1852). Practiced law and entered politics both in his native New Hampshire and in Massachusetts. In Congress he was known as a great orator and as a representative of the business interests of New England. He opposed many issues of the day: high tariff, cheap land, federal construction of internal improvements, the establishment of the second Bank, and slavery. Basically he was a nationalist although he sometimes let the prejudices of New England obscure his feelings.

Martin Van Buren (1782-1862). A New York politician who never took a position if he could avoid doing so. Therefore, it is difficult to determine his views on the issues of the 1820's, except to say that he did not oppose internal improvements, and that he did not conspicuously fight the rechartering of the Bank. Van Buren later became Vice President under Jackson and then President.

SOUTHERN LEADERS

William H. Crawford (1772-1834). A Georgia conservative who served in the House, the Senate, as minister to France, and as Secretary of the Treasury under Monroe. He favored rechartering the Bank and supported a mildly protective tariff, although he was predisposed toward a states'-rights position. His presidential ambitions were struck down in 1824 when he suffered a crippling stroke.

John C. Calhoun (1782-1850). A South Carolina politician who in the early 1820's was a true nationalist. He supported the national bank, a moderate tariff, and federal support of internal improvements. He served as congressman, as secretary of war under Monroe, and as Vice President under both Adams and Jackson. He was better known for his extreme states'-rights position which he later proclaimed as senator from South Carolina.

WESTERN LEADERS

Henry Clay (1777-1852). Practiced law in Kentucky and then became a congressman, serving as Speaker of the House, from 1811 to 1820 and from 1823 to 1825. His nationalist view was bound up in a program he called the American System. This plan called for a program of federal aid in the construction of roads and canals, a protective tariff, and a national bank.

Thomas Hart Benton (1782-1858). Senator for 30 years from Missouri, who favored free homesteads for pioneers and an extensive federally sponsored internal improvements program. He opposed the Bank, and although personally opposed to the tariff, he voted for it to protect Missouri's lead and furs.

William Henry Harrison (1773-1841). A military man who served in the House and the Senate for Ohio. During the Panic of 1819 he took an anti-Bank and a pro-high-tariff stand. He later became President, dying after one month in office.

Andrew Jackson (1767-1845). A politician and military hero from Tennessee who did not express his views on most issues. His forceful personality and military reputation were his chief assets.

NORTHERN CULTURE

Architecture.

Charles Bulfinch (1763-1844). An architect who studied in England and then developed his own "Federal" style, which was used most extensively in Boston.

Literature.

North American Review. A journal which published the works of American literary talent. Its purpose was to raise the standards of American literature and criticism; it existed from 1815 to 1939.

James Fenimore Cooper (1789-1851). A novelist who wrote a series of stories about Indians and settlers on the frontier, such as The Spy and The Last of the Mohicans. His stories reflected the romanticism of the early 19th century in which civilization was portrayed as corrupt, and the Indian and his wilderness as noble and natural.

Washington Irving (1783-1859). An author who first won acclaim in New York by contributing to the Salmagundi Papers and by writing a comical History of New York. He then moved to Europe (1815-1832) where he wrote his most important book, The Sketch Book of Geoffrey Crayon, Gent, which included "Rip Van Winkle" and "The Legend of Sleepy Hollow."

Art.

John Singleton Copley (1738-1815). An artist who developed a successful career in Boston as a portrait painter of wealthy New Englanders. His technique was sometimes criticized, however, so in 1774 he moved to London and continued his painting there. Note the portrait of Sam Adams by Copley on p. 88.

Charles Willson Peale (1741-1827). An artist who helped found the Pennsylvania Academy of Fine Arts, and did much to encourage American painting. He also established in

Philadelphia a museum of natural history which contained fossils and stuffed animals. Note his painting on p. 241.

Gilbert Stuart (1755-1828). An American artist best known for his portraits of George Washington. See his portrait of John Randolph of Roanoke on p. 172.

Religion.

Second Great Awakening. A religious revival movement of the early 1800's. It was similar in its emotional approach to the original Great Awakening of the 1740's. The Second Great Awakening's most influential preacher was Charles Grandison Finney.

Unitarian Church. The liberal wing of the Congregational Church, which was particularly strong in New England. The American Unitarian Association was founded in 1825 under the leadership of William Ellery Channing. The movement got its name from the fact that its members rejected the Christian doctrine of the Trinity, that is, a three in one God - Father, Son, and Holy Spirit. The church had no set doctrine and took as its watchword "deeds not creeds." In 1961 the Unitarians merged with the Universalists to form the Unitarian Universalist Association.

SOUTHERN CULTURE

The South was predominantly rural, with only one major city, Charleston, South Carolina. The great slave-owners dominated society, although the African heritage also permeated the white culture. In religion, the Protestant churches of the South leaned toward authoritarian and emotional approaches.

WESTERN LIFE

The rapidly expanding West was primarily agricultural, although there were some growing cities such as New Orleans, Louisiana; Cincinnati, Ohio; Pittsburgh, Pennsylvania; and Lexington, Kentucky. Society was dominated by a feeling of equality and democracy, although westerners did not apply these ideals to Indians and blacks. Religion played an important role as Protestant sects established colleges and the emotional Second Great Awakening swept through with special force.

SECTIONALISM AND POLITICS

Missouri.

1819, Missouri Enabling Act. Introduced in Congress to provide for the admission of Missouri as a state. It did not pass.

Tallmadge Amendment. Introduced by New York Congressman James Tallmadge as an amendment to the Missouri Enabling Act. Its purpose was to prohibit more slaves being brought into Missouri, and to provide that all slaves born there after it became a state would be freed at the age of 25. The vote was along sectional lines, and the amendment passed the House but was rejected by the Senate.

1820, Missouri Compromise. Missouri was admitted to the Union as a slave state, Maine separated from Massachusetts and entered as a free state, thus preserving the balance of free and slave states. Congress also adopted the proposal of Senator Jesse B. Thomas of Illinois whereby slavery was prohibited in all other parts of the Louisiana Purchase north of 36° 30' north latitude, that is, north of Missouri's southern boundary.

Election of 1824. The second time a presidential election was thrown into the House of Representatives. There were four candidates, all members of the Democratic-Republican party: Andrew Jackson, John Quincy Adams, William Crawford, and Henry Clay. Jackson got the largest number of votes in the Electoral College, but not a majority, so the top three, Jackson, Adams, and Crawford, were voted on in the House of Representatives, each state having one vote. Henry Clay asked those states which had supported him to vote for John Quincy Adams, and Adams won. Jackson felt that the election had been stolen from him, and immediately began campaigning for the 1828 race.

--"corrupt bargain." President Adams appointed Henry Clay as Secretary of State, the position which had traditionally been the "stepping stone to the presidency." The defeated Jackson then cried that there had been a "corrupt bargain" made, whereby Clay used his influence to get Adams elected, and in return, he got the Cabinet position plus possible support in the future for the presidency.

JOHN QUINCY ADAMS (1767-1848), 6th President

--Born in Massachusetts, graduated from Harvard, and practiced law in Boston.
--Served as Minister to the Netherlands, Prussia, and Russia.
--Federalist Senator from Massachusetts, then switched his party affiliation to Democratic-Republican.
--Helped negotiate the Treaty of Ghent.
--Secretary of State under Monroe where he negotiated the Transcontinental Treaty and helped write the Monroe Doctrine.
--President (1825-1829).
--Helped form a new political party called the National Republican party.
--Member of the House of Representatives (1831-1848) where he verbally opposed the expansion of slavery.

1828, Tariff of Abominations. Northern and western agricultural interests were able to push through a bill placing high duties on raw wool, hemp, flax, fur, and liquor. The southerners unsuccessfully tried to block the bill and in their anger dubbed it the Tariff of Abominations.

1828, South Carolina Exposition and Protest. Written by John C. Calhoun to condemn the tariff and the economic ruin it could bring to the south. The essay is significant because in it Calhoun presented the idea that since the states had created the Union, they should have the final say as to the meaning of the Constitution. If a special state convention, representing the people, decided that an act of Congress violated the Constitution, that state could "nullify" the law within its boundaries. Four years later South Carolina tried to nullify the tariff.

OTHER TERMS TO IDENTIFY

William Jones. President of the second Bank of the United States from 1816 to 1819. Jones' easygoing management practices and the Bank's overextension of credit caused the institution trouble when the Panic of 1819 struck, and Jones resigned.

Langdon Cheves. Second president of the second Bank of the United States. He was considered a conservative, and he cut back on credit extended at a time when, because of the panic, easy credit was needed. The Bank reached a low point in public favor.

Albany Regency. A term for the political machine in the state of New York which was controlled by Martin Van Buren.

Tapping Reeve's law school. Founded in Litchfield, Connecticut, in 1784, its graduates included a number of men prominent in public affairs. John C. Calhoun was one.

Benjamin West (1738-1820). An American born artist who moved to Europe in 1760 and spent most of his life painting and teaching in England. He was influential on American painting of the period because a number of young artists from the United States studied under him, including John Singleton Copley, Charles Willson Peale, and Gilbert Stuart.

James McGready (1758-1817). A Presbyterian minister whose preaching at revivals in Kentucky helped spark the Second Great Awakening. The gatherings for his revivals have sometimes been considered the forerunners of camp meetings.

camp meeting. An outdoor religious meeting which was generally sponsored by an evangelical sect, such as the Baptists and the Methodists, on the American frontier. The meeting lasted for several days, was led by one or more preachers, and the emotionally-charged audiences sometimes shouted, shook, and rolled on the ground after their "conversion" experiences. In a modified form, camp or tent meetings continue to serve a social and religious function in rural areas.

GLOSSARY

abomination. Something that elicits great dislike or loathing.

brimstone. An obsolete word for sulfur. James McGready, the preacher, convinced his congregations to lead Christian lives by describing a lake of fire and brimstone, that is, hell, which awaited them if they did not.

classical studies. The study of ancient Greek and Roman literature. Almost all colleges before the 20th century emphasized classical studies, and frequently an admission requirement was the ability to read Latin and Greek.

cultural assimilation. The process in which a minority or immigrant group adopts the characteristics of the culture or country in which they live. The question of how culturally assimilated African slaves and their descendants became in the South is still being studied.

mastodon. A large, elephant-like animal, now extinct. In 1801 Charles Willson Peale conducted a scientific expedition on a New York farm to bring up the bones of a prehistoric mastodon. Note his painting of the event on p. 241.

millennium. In Christian doctrine, the millennium is a thousand year period of holiness in which Christ is to rule on earth. Charles Grandison Finney, an outstanding preacher of the Second Great Awakening, felt that the millennium would come soon if men would only heed the teachings of Christianity and behave honestly toward one another.

rhetoric. The study of elements used in literature or in public speaking, such as content, structure, or style. It is also the art of oratory, that is, the persuasive use of language to influence the thoughts and actions of others. Rhetoric was a standard course of study in colleges of the early 1800's.

rote learning. Learning by memorizing, repeating facts without necessarily understanding them. Rote learning was the accepted method used by all educational institutions of the early 1800's.

subscription library. A library to which a member paid annual dues in order to use it. The money was used for maintenance and for buying new books, at a time when cities did not give money for this service. Most larger towns in the United States had subscription libraries before 1815.

yeoman farmer. A term used to refer to small independent farmers. William H. Crawford, Georgia politician, generally spoke for the large planters and against the interests of the yeoman farmer.

DEFINE THE FOLLOWING, USING THE DICTIONARY IF NECESSARY

alchemy
amalgam
anthropologically
charismatic
cogency
deracinated
hyperbolically
sedulous
venal
vermilion

SAMPLE QUESTIONS

MULTIPLE CHOICE

1. Henry Clay's "American System" called for:
   a. high-priced public lands.
   b. the abolition of the national bank.
   c. a protective tariff, federal internal improvements, and a national bank.
   d. the admission of Missouri as a slave state.

2. Three of these usually characterized frontier communities. Which did not?
   a. individualism.
   b. social classes.
   c. democracy.
   d. optimism.

3. Frontier camp meetings had as their chief purpose the:
   a. holding of religious services.
   b. building of houses and barns for new settlers.
   c. holding of elections.
   d. organizing of wagon trains for migration to the West.

4. Clay's appointment as Secretary of State in 1825 led to:
   a. a decrease of partisan bitterness.
   b. a revival of the Federalist party.
   c. charges of corrupt bargaining on the part of Adams and Clay.
   d. a weakening of the Electoral College.

5. The status of slavery in the Louisiana Territory was

affected by the:
a. Maine Compromise.
b. Missouri Compromise.
c. American System.
d. Jim Crow laws.

MATCHING

1.	Charles Willson Peale	a.	a minister whose preaching helped start the Second Great Awakening.
2.	Daniel Webster	b.	a New York politician who never took a firm stand on the issues of the day.
3.	James McGready	c.	an author who wrote stories about the American frontier.
4.	James Fenimore Cooper	d.	an artist who also opened a museum of natural history.
5.	Martin Van Buren	e.	a Massachusetts politician who represented the business interests of New England.

ANSWERS
<u>MULTIPLE</u> CHOICE: c,b,a,c,b. MATCHING: 1-d,2-e,3-a,4-c,
5-b.

Portfolio 3
Tocqueville's America

PORTFOLIO CHECKLIST

Alexis de Tocqueville (1805-1859). A French liberal politician and writer who came to the United States in 1831 on a government mission. He and his companion, Gustave de Beaumont, were supposed to study the American penal system but their journeys gave them a much broader scope on life in America.

Democracy in America. Written and published by Tocqueville in 1835, first in French, then in English and other translations. It described his impressions of the United States and is considered a classic in political literature. He discussed the advantages and shortcomings of the democratic political and social system which in Europe was still considered an experiment. Tocqueville attempted to justify democracy and predicted its survival and success. The book continues to be relevant because many of his observations about America and American life are still very much in evidence today.

Tocequeville's impressions of America.

--A visit to New York illustrated that America was a business society, bent on the acquisition of riches.
--The wealthy were concerned with status symbols.
--The country had an extensive network of communications, at that time consisting primarily of stagecoaches and steamboats.
--The frontier accustomed people to change and optimism about what the future might bring them.
--A visit to Cincinnati showed how rapidly cities grew, often with no real system or plan.
--Southerners considered physical labor degrading, as a result of the slavery in their midst. Tocqueville appreciated southern charm and hospitality while at the same time predicting that the South would end "by being

dominated by the North."

--In family relations, parents did not exert strong authority, and treated all their children equally, whether male or female, first-born or last.

--Americans were "joiners," forming clubs and associations for almost every purpose.

--A certain restlessness was evident; people were on the move. There was a good deal of physical and social mobility.

--Religion had an influence on the morals and conduct of the people.

--An interest in formal education was evident, although people also learned through participating in government and by reading newspapers.

--In Tocqueville's opinion, the politicians in Washington lacked a sense of high purpose, but nonetheless he sensed a bright future for the United States.

Which of the above are still true today?

GLOSSARY

esquire. A member of the English gentry ranking just below a knight. The term was also used as a title of courtesy after a man's name, and was considered somewhat pretentious. Beaumont wrote that in New York many of the so-called champions of equality called themselves "honorable esquires."

broadside. A large sheet of paper printed on one side. Often it is used for advertising or for propaganda. An engraving from a mailstage broadside is pictured on p. P3-VII.

bateau a vapeur americain. French for American steamboat. Tocqueville and Beaumont used this craft while traveling; one is pictured on p. P3-VI.

meteorologist. A scientist who deals with the phenomena of the atmosphere, especially weather and weather conditions. A drawing on p. P3-XX shows meteorologist James Pollard Epsy delivering a lyceum lecture in New York in 1841.

DEFINE THE FOLLOWING, USING THE DICTIONARY IF NECESSARY

antipodes
centrifugal
centripetal
coteries
prodigious
vortex

10

The Age of Jackson

CHAPTER CHECKLIST

ANDREW JACKSON (1767-1845), 7th President

- --Born in South Carolina, moved to Tennessee where he practiced law.
- --Nicknamed "Old Hickory," and his Tennessee plantation was called the Hermitage.
- --Served as congressman and senator from Tennessee, and as a judge on the Tennessee Supreme Court.
- --The hero of the Battle of New Orleans in the War of 1812.
- --Invaded Florida during the Seminole War of 1818, and in 1821 was appointed military governor of Florida.
- --Won the popular vote in the presidential race of 1824, but lost the election in the House of Representatives.
- --Formed a new political party, which he called the Democratic Party.
- --President (1829-1837).

THE JACKSON ERA

Spoils system. Practice by which political party supporters were rewarded with government jobs. As William Marcy of New York proclaimed in 1831, "To the victors belong the spoils." Other presidents had appointed political friends to offices, but Jackson did so on a larger scale, replacing about 20 per cent. He used a democratic justification for his actions - by "rotating" jobholders more citizens had an opportunity to participate in self-government.

Kitchen Cabinet. A group of unofficial advisors upon whom Jackson relied for advice, particularly between 1829 and 1831. The only member who was also part of the regular Cabinet was Martin Van Buren, who was secretary of state during Jackson's first term.

Webster-Hayne debate in the Senate.

--Senator Foot of Connecticut suggested the sale of public land should be sharply reduced.
--Senator Benton of Missouri denounced this proposal as a plot by the eastern manufacturers to stop the westward migration of their workers.
--Senator Hayne of South Carolina supported Benton and suggested that the West and the South work together to obtain cheap land and low tariffs.
--Senator Webster of Massachusetts, who supported the northeastern manufacturers, spoke against Hayne's ideas.
--1830, Webster-Hayne debate. Started as a discussion of federal land policies but ended as a debate of states'-rights versus the power of the national government. Hayne, voicing Vice President Calhoun's views, spoke for states'-rights while Webster, in a two-day oration, denounced nullification as close to treason. The ultimate effect prevented a West-South alliance.

Indian problems. Jackson demonstrated a states'-rights position by encouraging Georgia to ignore or "nullify" a Supreme Court decision concerning Indians.

--Cherokee Nation. A tribe of Indians who tried to hold on to their land in Georgia by adopting white ways. They took up farming and cattle-raising, developed a written language, wrote a constitution, and set up a state within a state in Georgia.
--1828. Georgia passed a law declaring all Cherokee laws void and the region part of Georgia.
--1832, Worcester v. Georgia. Corn Tassel, a Cherokee, was convicted of murder in a Georgia court, but he appealed the case all the way to the Supreme Court by stating that the murder had taken place in Cherokee territory. The Supreme Court upheld Corn Tassel's argument, and declared Georgia's actions unconstitutional. Jackson, however, did not agree with the decision of Chief Justice John Marshall and his Court about letting a separate nation exist within a state, and indicated that the executive branch would not enforce the court ruling. Therefore, Georgia ignored the decision of Worcester v. Georgia and hanged Corn Tassel.
--1835. A minority of Cherokees was bribed to sign a treaty surrendering their lands and was driven west to Oklahoma in a forced march known as the "Trail of Tears."

Nullification crisis. Jackson took a nationalist rather than a states'-rights position when South Carolina tried to nullify the tariff.

--1828. The high Tariff of Abominations went into effect, and the South Carolina legislature passed eight resolutions denouncing it as unfair and unconstitutional.
--1828. South Carolina Exposition and Protest was written by John C. Calhoun to oppose the tariff and to present an argument for a state's right to reject or "nullify" an act of Congress.

--1832. Another tariff was passed which was also unsatisfactory to the South, particularly South Carolina.
--November, 1832. South Carolina elected a special convention which passed an Ordinance of Nullification, prohibiting the collection of tariff duties in the state after February 1, 1833. In January this deadline was postponed pending the outcome of the new tariff debate.
--January, 1833, Force Bill. Introduced to authorize President Jackson to call up troops if necessary to collect the tariff. The bill became law on March 1, but by then a compromise had been reached.
--March, 1833. A compromise tariff worked out by Henry Clay and John C. Calhoun passed Congress and provided for a gradual reduction over a ten-year period.
--March 15, 1833. South Carolina convention reassembled and repealed the Nullification Ordinance, but in order to save face, on the same day it adopted a new ordinance nullifying the Force Act.

Bank War.

--1816. Second Bank of the United States was chartered for a twenty-year period.
--1823. Nicholas Biddle, a wealthy Philadelphian, became president of the Bank.
--1832. Congress passed a bill to recharter the Bank, four years before its charter would have expired. This was a political move designed by the National Republicans to create an issue for the 1832 presidential campaign.
--1832. Jackson vetoed the rechartering of the Bank, calling the institution "the Monster." Although the Bank continued in existence until 1836, Jackson won the "Bank War" by having federal income deposited in state banks, while he continued to draw money out of the national bank.
--1836. Specie Circular provided that purchasers must pay for public land in gold or silver, rather than in bank notes. It was an effort by President Jackson to check inflation and land speculation. But it also set off a chain of events which led to the financial Panic of 1837.

POLITICAL PARTY ALIGNMENTS

MAJOR POLITICAL PARTIES
and approximate dates

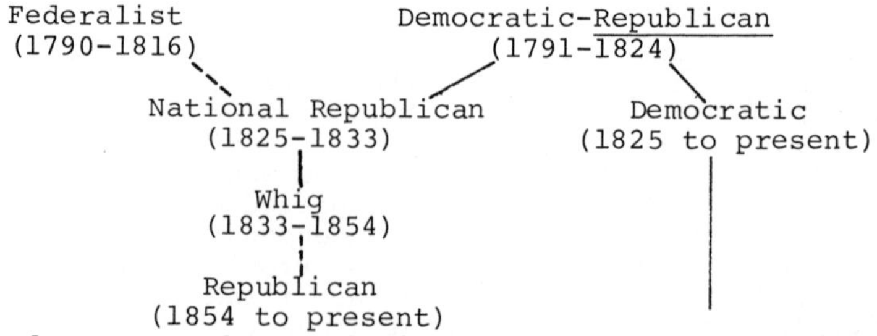

---denotes a close relationship, but not direct evolution.
——denotes direct evolution.

Democratic Party. After the election of 1824, in which all candidates considered themselves Republicans (or Democratic-Republicans as Jefferson had originally called the party), the followers of President Adams called themselves National Republicans. Jackson and his followers claimed to be the true political descendants of Jefferson and they went back to the original name of the party, calling themselves Democrats. They shared some characteristics:

--personally loyal to Andrew Jackson.
--opposed the second Bank of the United States.
--supported states'-rights, but also felt the union was supreme, as Jackson demonstrated in the nullification crisis.
--favored internal improvements, but felt they should be paid for by the state, as was evident in the Maysville Road veto.
--believed that the ordinary man was capable of performing the duties of most public offices. This view contributed to rotation in office, or the spoils system.
--championed a belief in the equality of all white men, which caused immigrants, Catholics, and other minority groups to join the party.

Whig Party. Composed of the opponents of Andrew Jackson, whom they referred to as "King Andrew." They took their name from the Whig Party in England which traditionally supported a strong Parliament rather than a strong monarch. During the Revolution the Patriots had also called themselves Whigs, referring to their opposition to King George III.

--former Federalists and National Republicans began to call themselves Whigs in 1834.
--leaders included Henry Clay, Daniel Webster, and John C. Calhoun.
--favored the second Bank of the United States.
--wanted a national approach to economic problems, such as internal improvements.
--supported by the extreme states'-rights followers of Calhoun.
--included people of education, culture and social position.
--supported by evangelical religious groups predisposed to favor strong governments.
--had difficulty agreeing on anything other than opposition to Jackson.

VAN BUREN'S POLICIES

--fought the Bank of the United States as a monopoly, but also opposed irresponsible state banks.
--believed in public construction of internal improvements, but favored state rather than national programs.
--never committed himself on the tariff issue.
--generally followed states'-rights rather than nationalist policies.

--took a "hands-off" approach to the depression which followed the Panic of 1837.

--supported the Independent Treasury Act which Congress passed in 1840. It called for the construction of government-owned vaults in various parts of the country, where all federal revenues could be stored until needed, rather than keeping them in state banks. To insure absolute safety, all payments to the government were to be made in hard cash.

MARTIN VAN BUREN (1782-1862), 8th President

--Born in New York and studied law.
--Called the "Red Fox" and the "Little Magician."
--State senator and attorney general in New York.
--Leader of the Albany Regency, the Democratic party machine of New York.
--United States Senator.
--Won governorship of New York in 1828 and resigned to become Jackson's secretary of state.
--Vice President under Jackson (1833-1837).
--President (1837-1841).

ELECTION OF 1840

--Democrats nominated the incumbent, Martin Van Buren, but the years of depression and the stories told by his opponents led to his defeat. Van Buren was pictured by the Whigs as an extravagant man luxuriating in Washington, D.C., at the expense of the people.

--Whigs nominated General William Henry Harrison, the well-educated son of a former governor of Virginia, and pictured him as a man of the people who lived in a log cabin and drank hard cider. They appealed to the western vote by recalling his Indian fighting days with the slogan "Tippecanoe and Tyler too." John Tyler of Virginia was the Vice Presidential candidate.

--General Harrison and the Whigs won the election by using the same appeal to the common man that the Democrats had used in electing Jackson.

WILLIAM HENRY HARRISON (1773-1841), 9th President

--Born in Virginia but moved West and became an Indian fighter.
--Delegate to Congress from the Northwest Territory.
--Governor of Indiana Territory from 1800 to 1813.
--Led a force against an Indian encampment at Tippecanoe in 1811 and won the nickname "Old Tippecanoe."
--Moved to Ohio and represented that state first in the House and then in the Senate.
--President (1841).
--Died from pneumonia on April 4, exactly one month after he had been inaugurated. He was the first president to die while in office.

OTHER TERMS TO IDENTIFY

Congressional caucus. The members of Congress met, by party, to select the presidential candidate for their party. This system came to an end before 1828. In that year Jackson and Adams were put forward by state legislatures. Soon the system of nomination by national party convention, such as we have today, was adopted.

pocket veto. In order for a bill to become a law the president must sign it within ten days or it goes into effect, even without his signature. He may also veto the bill and send it back to the house where it originated. Within the last ten days of a congressional session, the President may simply "put the bill in his pocket," neither signing nor vetoing it, and it has the same effect as a veto. Jackson not only used the veto more than all his predecessors combined, but he was also the first to use the pocket veto.

1828-1829, Eaton affair. Senator John Eaton of Tennessee, a bachelor, lived in a boarding house in Washington, D.C., and had an affair with the innkeeper's daughter, Peggy O'Neal Timberlake. Mrs. Timberlake was married to a Navy purser who was frequently away on sea duty. When her husband died in 1828, she married Eaton, then the newly-appointed secretary of war. Other Cabinet wives refused to accept Mrs. Eaton socially; they were led in their snubbings by the Vice President's wife, Floride Calhoun. Martin Van Buren, a widower, was the only Cabinet member who paid his respects to the couple. President Jackson, remembering the social slights to his own wife, Rachel, was furious at the other Cabinet members. This fracas had political repercussions in that it marked the beginnings of John C. Calhoun's decline in favor and the ascendancy of Van Buren, who succeeded Calhoun as Jackson's Vice President. The affair also caused Jackson to turn more to his personal friends, that is, the Kitchen Cabinet, for advice.

1830, Maysville Road veto. Congress passed a bill to construct a turnpike from Maysville to Lexington, Kentucky. Jackson vetoed the bill, claiming that the road was intrastate rather than interstate, and therefore the state should pay for it, not the federal government. This action illustrated a states'-rights rather than a nationalist approach to internal improvements.

pet banks. After Jackson vetoed the rechartering of the second Bank of the United States in 1832, he began to phase out the Bank by depositing new federal money in certain state banks. This procedure was handled by his newly-appointed secretary of the treasury, Roger B. Taney, who deposited the money in state banks which were politically sympathetic to Jackson. These favored banks became known as "pet banks."

Locofoco. The name of the radical wing of Jackson's Democratic Party which particularly championed the rights of the common man. A locofoco was a type of match, and the name was first used when a group of New York Jacksonians used these matches to light candles when a conservative faction had tried to break up their meeting by turning off the gaslights.

Washington Globe. The Washington newspaper which actively supported Jackson's policies. The paper's motto was "That government is best which governs least."

GLOSSARY

daguerreotype. An early type of photograph which became popular in the 1840's. It was produced on a silver plate or a copper plate covered with silver and developed by mercury vapor. Note the daguerreotype of Martin Van Buren on p. 274.

Haman. A favored minister in the court of Xerxes I, or Ahasuerus as he is called in the Bible, who was king of Persia in the fifth century B.C. Haman commanded that all Jews in the kingdom be put to death, but Queen Esther interceded for her people and Haman was hanged on the gallows which had been set up for Mordecai, a Jew whom Haman particularly hated. Jackson threatened Calhoun that if South Carolina attempted to nullify a law he would "hang him as high as Haman."

hard cider. Cider is made from the juice of apples. When it ferments, and thus has an alcoholic content, it is called hard cider.

latchstring. A cord or string on a latch, either hanging on the outside of the door so that the latch can be raised from the outside, or drawn inside to prevent people from entering unless the door is opened from the inside. In the 1840 election, the Whigs stated that their candidate lived in a log cabin where the latchstring was always out, that is, welcoming everyone.

lithograph. A print made by the process of lithography. Lithography is a printing process in which the image to be printed is drawn on a flat surface, such as stone, or more recently on zinc or aluminum. The surface is treated so that the drawing will retain ink and the non-image area is treated to repel ink. Note the lithograph on p. 264.

South Sea Bubble. The popular name in England for the financial speculation in the South Sea Company, which was formed in 1711 and failed disastrously in 1720.

Needing money to finance the War of Spanish Succession, the British government allowed the company to assume the national debt in exchange for an annual interest payment from the government plus a monopoly of British trade with the islands of the South Seas and South America. The price of the stock rose out of all proportion to its earnings in trade, and eventually the stock collapsed and the bubble burst.

DEFINE THE FOLLOWING, USING THE DICTIONARY IF NECESSARY

commensurate
demagoguery
equivocate
expiate
grandiloquence
hydra
inexorable
masthead (newspaper)
niggardliness
plutocrats

SAMPLE QUESTIONS

MULTIPLE CHOICE

1. What was Andrew Jackson's attitude toward the spoils system?
    a. that civil service laws should be strengthened.
    b. that the spoils system was bad, but he could not do anything about it.
    c. that rotation in office was a good thing.
    d. that only highly educated persons should hold jobs in the government.

2. The South Carolina Ordinance of Nullification of 1832 expressed the ideas of:
    a. Daniel Webster
    b. Andrew Jackson
    c. John Adams
    d. John C. Calhoun

3. One result of the Peggy Eaton affair was:
    a. a victory for the Calhoun faction.
    b. a serious breach between Jackson and Calhoun.
    c. the resignation of the Kitchen Cabinet.
    d. Van Buren's fall from power.

4. Jackson's chief weapon in the "Bank War" was:
    a. the removal of Biddle from office.
    b. the removal of government deposits.
    c. the contraction of credit.
    d. the Specie Circular.

5. Who of these defended the view that the Union was formed by the whole people of the United States and not by the states?

a. John C. Calhoun
b. Thomas Jefferson
c. Robert Hayne
d. Daniel Webster

TRUE-FALSE

1. In Worcester v. Georgia, Jackson encouraged the state of Georgia not to obey the Supreme Court ruling.

2. Jackson vetoed the Maysville Road Bill because he thought the state of Kentucky should finance it.

3. In 1832 South Carolina tried to nullify an embargo.

4. Nicholas Biddle was a member of Jackson's Kitchen Cabinet.

5. In the "log cabin-hard cider" campaign of 1840, the Democratic candidate won.

ANSWERS
MULTIPLE CHOICE: c,d,b,b,d. TRUE-FALSE: T,T,F,F,F.

11
Expansion and Slavery

CHAPTER CHECKLIST

JOHN TYLER (1790-1862), 10th President

--Born in Virginia.
--Member of the House of Representatives (1817-1821).
--Governor of Virginia (1825-1827).
--United States Senator (1827-1836).
--Member of the Jeffersonian Republican Party, then the Jacksonian Democratic Party, then the Whig Party.
--Vice President under William Henry Harrison during his one month in office.
--President (1841-1845).

TYLER AS PRESIDENT

--States'-rights view of the Constitution.
--Opposed the Bank, a high tariff, and federal internal improvements, all of which were supported by Henry Clay and the Northern Whigs.
--Cast out by his own party, he unsuccessfully tried to build a party of his own.

1841, Distribution Act. A measure supported by Henry Clay, whereby the proceeds from the sale of public land went to the states. This act was designed to improve the financial situation of the states, but Clay also wanted to lower the amount in the national treasury so as to justify raising the tariff. The Distribution Act was repealed the next year.

1841, Pre-emption Act. Legalized the right of squatters to occupy unsurveyed public land and to buy it later at $1.25 an acre without bidding for it at auction.

PROBLEMS WITH ENGLAND

Maine - New Brunswick boundary dispute. Became critical in 1838-1839 when Canadians began cutting timber in the Aroostook Valley which was claimed by the United States. This action led to the Aroostook "war," a bloodless, undeclared war that threatened Anglo-American relations.

Slavery and the African slave trade. Problems created because although both England and the United States had abolished slave trading, the United States did not actively enforce its prohibition.

--1841, Creole incident. The brig Creole sailed from Virginia toward New Orleans with a cargo of slaves, making a legal voyage from one state to another. But the slaves seized the ship and put into the British port of Nassau in the Bahama Islands in the Caribbean. The British, who had abolished slavery in 1834, arrested the ring leaders but freed most of the Negroes, despite United States protests.

1842, Webster-Ashburton Treaty.

--Worked out by Secretary of State Daniel Webster and Britain's Alexander Baring, whose title was Lord Ashburton.
--Set the present Maine-Canada boundary with the United States giving up 5,000 square miles in northern Maine.
--England ceded 6,500 square miles between Lake Superior and Lake of the Woods, which later was found to contain the valuable Mesabi iron deposits.
--Agreed to suppress the slave trade by maintaining separate but cooperating naval squadrons off the African coast.

TEXAS

--1530's. Cabeza de Vaca crossed Texas and claimed the area for Spain.
--1530's - 1821. A colony of Spain.
--1821 - 1836. Part of the Republic of Mexico.
--1836 - 1845. Independent Republic of Texas.
--1845. Annexed by the United States.

Stephen F. Austin. Received a grant from Mexico to bring American settlers into Texas. They began arriving in 1821. By 1830, 20,000 had come, bringing their slaves and planting cotton.

Alamo. Colonel William B. Travis led the Texans against General Santa Anna's Mexican army at the Battle of the Alamo in San Antonio. The Mexican army was victorious on March 6, 1836, and all survivors were killed, including Travis, Davy Crockett, and Jim Bowie. The battle marked a low point in the morale of the Texas forces, but also provided the rallying cry "Remember the Alamo."

Battle of San Jacinto. On April 21, 1836, the Texans scored an outstanding victory over the Mexican army at the San Jacinto River near present day Houston. The Texans were led by Sam Houston, a former congressman and governor of Tennessee, who later became president of the Republic of Texas.

MANIFEST DESTINY

A term used to describe the spirit of continental expansionism which existed in the United States in the 1840's. The phrase was coined by a Democratic editor named John L. O'Sullivan in July, 1845. He warned against foreign powers, namely Great Britain, saying it was "the fulfillment of our manifest destiny to overspread the continent allotted by Providence for the free development of our early multiplying millions."

OREGON

--1778. Claimed by Captain James Cook for England.
--1792. The American captain Robert Gray sailed up the Columbia River.
--1805. Lewis and Clark visited the area.
--1818. Joint occupation by England and the United States.
--1840's. "Oregon fever" hit and pioneers trekked over the Oregon Trail to settle the area.
--1846. United States and England agreed to divide the territory along the 49th parallel.

Oregon Trail. The route from Independence, Missouri, to the mouth of the Columbia River on the Pacific coast which was the main highway for pioneers to Oregon. The trail was 2,000 miles long, and it took about 5 months to make the trip.

ANNEXATION

Annexation of Oregon. Arranged by treaty between Great Britain and the United States in 1846. Some Americans had wanted all the territory and used the slogan "54° 40' or fight." But President Polk agreed on the 49th parallel, following that line from the Rockies to Puget Sound. Britain received Vancouver Island and the right to navigate the Columbia River. Both nations retained free use of the Strait of Juan de Fuca.

Election of 1844. Henry Clay was the Whig candidate and James K. Polk was the Democratic nominee. The Democrats' slogan was the "reannexation of Texas and the reoccupation of Oregon," while Clay and the Whigs hedged on the expansionist policy. There was a third party in the race, the

Liberty party, an anti-slavery group first organized in 1840 whose candidate was James G. Birney. The election was close but the Democrat Polk won.

1845, Annexation of Texas. Tyler interpreted the election as a mandate for expansion, and asked Congress to pass a joint resolution annexing Texas before he left office.

--Texas entered the Union as a slave state in December, 1845.
--As many as four new states could be carved from her territory, but only with her approval.
--Texas retained title to all public lands within its boundaries.
--Texas accepted full responsibility for debts incurred while an independent republic.

JAMES K. POLK (1795-1849), 11th President

--Born in North Carolina and practiced law in Tennessee.
--Served in state legislature of Tennessee.
--Member of the House of Representatives (1825-1839) and elected Speaker of the House in 1835.
--President (1845-1849).

WAR WITH MEXICO

John Slidell (1793-1871). Sent to Mexico on a diplomatic mission from December, 1845 to March, 1846. Mexico owed $2 million in claims to American citizens and Slidell was authorized to cancel the debt in exchange for Mexico's diplomatically recognizing the annexation of Texas and accepting the Rio Grande River rather than the Nueces River as the southern border. Slidell was also empowered by President Polk to offer $5 million to buy New Mexico and $25 million for California. The Mexican government refused to negotiate with Slidell and he returned to the United States, convinced that military tactics rather than diplomacy would be necessary.

General Zachary Taylor (1784-1850). Known as "Old Rough and Ready," went to Texas in July, 1845 and camped on the Nueces River, near Corpus Christi. After the failure of Slidell's mission in March, 1846, he advanced to the Rio Grande and built Fort Texas, later named Fort Brown, across the Rio Grande from the Mexican town of Matamoros. When a Mexican force crossed the river into territory which Mexico also claimed and attacked an American patrol, the United States found the excuse it had been looking for. "War exists," General Taylor wired to President Polk.

May 13, 1846. Congress declared war on Mexico.

President Polk's three-pronged design for the war.

--Clear the Mexicans from Texas and occupy northern Mexico. To accomplish this General Taylor marched his troops through south Texas and into northern Mexico, culminating in a victory at Buena Vista. Note the map "The Mexican War" on p. 294.
--Take possession of California and New Mexico. These areas were taken in separate actions by settlers at Sonoma; Captain John C. Frémont at Monterey, California; Commodore John D. Sloat at Monterey and San Francisco; and General Stephen Kearny who took Santa Fe, New Mexico, and then marched to California.
--March on Mexico City and force authorities to sign an acceptable peace. General Winfield Scott landed an army at Veracruz, defeated a large Mexican force at Cerro Gordo, spent the summer at Puebla, and then took Mexico City. In personality Scott was somewhat pompous and was known as "Old Fuss and Feathers." After the war he was nominated for the presidency by the Whig Party in 1852, but was defeated.

Nicholas Trist. Chief clerk of the State Department who was sent to Mexico to accompany Scott's army and act as peace commissioner after the fall of Mexico City. The city fell in September, 1847, but because of unstable conditions in the government, Trist could not begin negotiations until January, 1848. Meanwhile President Polk, unable to understand the delay, recalled him. Trist ignored the order, negotiated the treaty, and sent it back to Washington with a newspaperman. Furious that Trist had disobeyed orders, Polk accepted the treaty but fired Trist from his State Department job without paying him for his mission. It was not until 1870 that Congress finally awarded Trist his back salary.

1848, Treaty of Guadalupe Hidalgo.

--Mexico ceded New Mexico and Upper California to the United States.
--Mexico recognized the Rio Grande River as the southern boundary of Texas.
--United States paid Mexico $15 million.
--United States assumed claims of American citizens against Mexico which amounted to $3.25 million.

SLAVERY AND THE TERRITORIES

1846, Wilmot Proviso. A proposed amendment to an appropriations bill for the conduct of the Mexican War and the acquisition of Mexican territory. It was presented by David Wilmot, congressman from Pennsylvania, and stated that slavery should not be permitted in any territory gained from Mexico. The amendment passed the House twice but was defeated in the Senate.

The Proviso was countered by a series of resolutions introduced in the Senate by John C. Calhoun which argued that Congress had no right to bar slavery from any territory. These resolutions had no chance in the northern-dominated House of Representatives. The proposals were significant because they illustrated the growing debate over slavery in the western territories.

popular sovereignty. An alternative to the question of whether or not slavery should be allowed in the West. The answer was to let the people in the western territories decide for themselves. Senator Lewis Cass of Michigan put forward this idea by calling for the organization of new territories without mentioning slavery.

Compromise of 1850. Five separate bills pushed through Congress by Henry Clay and Stephen Douglas in an attempt to smooth the friction between the sections of the country, particularly with regard to the slavery issue.
--California entered the Union as a free state.
--New Mexico and Utah were organized as territories and could enter the Union later with or without slavery, that is, under popular sovereignty.
--Texas accepted a narrower western boundary in exchange for the United States government giving it $10 million to pay off the $10 million debt left over from its days as a republic.
--Slave trade, but not slavery, in Washington, D.C., was abolished as of January 1, 1851.
--Stricter Fugitive Slave law was passed in an attempt to end the abolitionist practice of aiding runaway slaves. Federal commissioners were appointed with the authority to pursue runaways and to return them to their owners in the South.

ZACHARY TAYLOR (1784-1850), 12th President

--Born in Virginia, grew up in Kentucky.
--Joined the army and became an Indian fighter in the Midwest and in Florida.
--Became a military hero during the Mexican War as a result of his victories at Monterrey and Buena Vista.
--President (1849-1850) - the last Whig to be elected to the Presidency.
--Died in office, succeeded by Millard Fillmore.

MILLARD FILLMORE (1800-1874), 13th President

--Born in New York and became a self-taught lawyer.
--Served one term (1833-1835) in the House of Representatives as a member of the Anti-Masonic Party and three terms (1837-1843) as a Whig.
--Vice President under Zachary Taylor (1849-1850).
--President (1850-1853).
--Unsuccessful candidate for president (1856) on the Know Nothing, or American, ticket.

OTHER TERMS TO IDENTIFY

Franklin map. During the peace negotiations in Paris to end the American Revolution, Benjamin Franklin had marked the boundary between Maine and Canada on a map with a heavy red line. The map disappeared, but Daniel Webster, wanting to settle the boundary dispute once again in 1842, simply fabricated a map of the area which he passed off as the original. Webster had someone mark the map along the boundary claimed by the British; then he showed the map to representatives of Massachusetts, which claimed Maine until 1820, so that they would give in to a settlement and thus avoid war. Ironically, the British had a true copy of the Franklin map, which showed that the whole area in dispute rightfully belonged to the United States.

General Stephen Kearny (1794-1848). A military officer who took Santa Fe, New Mexico, with little resistance in August of 1846 and then marched with some of his troops to join operations in San Diego and Los Angeles. Note map "The Mexican War" on p. 294.

Barnburners. Name given to radical Democrats in the 1840's, particularly the followers of Martin Van Buren. Conservative Democrats accused them of being willing to burn down their political "barn" in order to get rid of rats, that is, undesirable persons and policies, in the party. Barnburners were especially opposed to the extension of slavery in the territories. In 1848 they joined the Free-Soil Party to nominate Martin Van Buren for the presidency.

Free-Soil Party. Political party founded in 1848 and made up of Democratic Barnburners and members of the Liberty Party. The name of their party had nothing to do with free land; instead it referred to their desire to prohibit the extension of slavery into the territory acquired in the Mexican War. Free Soil meant free from slavery. The Party nominated ex-President Martin Van Buren in 1848, and by the early 1850's it dissolved, many of its members joining the new Republican party.

GLOSSARY

affidavit. A written declaration made under oath before a notary public or other authorized officer. The Fugitive Slave Act which was included in the Compromise of 1850 stated that a runaway slave was to be returned to his owner without jury trial merely upon the submission of an affidavit by the owner. The affidavit would be a sworn statement that the slave was his.

amour propre. Self esteem or self-respect. It is a French term which literally means self-love. General Winfield Scott and Nicholas Trist, each concerned with his amour propre, immediately disliked each other when they met in Mexico. Each was jealous of his own image and interests.

dark horse. Originally referred to a little known entrant in a horse race. The term has also come to mean a person who receives unexpected support as a candidate for the nomination at a political convention. Often the person is a compromise candidate, as for example Polk who was put forward to break the deadlock between Van Buren and Calhoun.

eyes of Argus. In Greek mythology Argus was a giant with a hundred eyes. One who looks with the eyes of Argus is watchful and alert. Southern congressmen had a tendency to watch over the institution of slavery with the eyes of Argus, ever ready to defend it.

fait accompli. A French term which literally means an accomplished fact. When General Taylor wrote President Polk about the 1846 skirmish on the Mexican war, Polk looked upon the matter as if war already existed, a fait accompli, even before Congress made an official declaration.

guava. A fruit with a yellow rind and pink flesh used for making jelly or preserves. When Nicholas Trist first arrived in Mexico, he and General Scott did not get along. But when Trist became ill, Scott sent him a jar of guava marmalade, and after that goodwill gesture they became friends.

higher law. The law of God. William Seward used this phrase referring to a law higher than the Constitution. Because the Constitution and the Fugitive Slave Law legalized the institution of slavery, Seward advocated disobeying them in this regard.

Mother Lode. A long vein of gold-bearing rock in California. It is a 110-mile belt which runs from Mariposa to Georgetown, California, and it was first exploited in 1849.

teetotaler. A person who abstains completely from drinking alcoholic beverages. Lewis Cass, who popularized the idea of popular sovereignty, circulated at Washington social functions pretending to drink, even though he was a teetotaler.

DEFINE THE FOLLOWING, USING THE DICTIONARY IF NECESSARY

adjudicate	intransigence
asperities	psychopathic

punctilious
salved
sectarian
sundered
surfeit
volubility

SAMPLE QUESTIONS

MULTIPLE CHOICE

1. Which is the correct chronological order in which the following places became parts of the United States?
   a. Texas, Oregon, California.
   b. Oregon, Texas, California.
   c. California, Oregon, Texas.
   d. Oregon, California, Texas.

2. The concept of Manifest Destiny is most closely associated with the administration of:
   a. Zachary Taylor.
   b. James K. Polk.
   c. John Tyler.
   d. William Henry Harrison.

3. When the war with Mexico began, a force of American troops was sent over the Santa Fe Trail to conquer the province of New Mexico and move on to California. These troops were led by:
   a. John C. Frémont.
   b. Zachary Taylor.
   c. Winfield Scott.
   d. Stephen W. Kearny.

4. Military heroes have been elected by the American people to the office of President many times, such as the hero of Buena Vista in the war with Mexico, who was:
   a. Winfield Scott.
   b. Millard Fillmore.
   c. Zachary Taylor.
   d. William Henry Harrison.

5. The South won its chief concession in that part of the Compromise of 1850 which concerned:
   a. slavery in New Mexico and Utah.
   b. slavery in the District of Columbia.
   c. fugitive slaves.
   d. the admission of a new state.

TRUE-FALSE

1. The Maine-Canada border dispute was settled by the 1842 Webster-Ashburton Treaty.

2. The Mexican War was opposed by members of the Whig Party.

3. The Pre-emption Act took money from the sale of public lands and gave it to the states.

4. The slogan "fifty-four forty or fight" was used in connection with the annexation of Texas.

5. The Free-Soil Party was concerned with the sale of public lands in the west.

<u>ANSWERS</u>

MULTIPLE CHOICE: a,b,d,c,c. TRUE-FALSE: T,T,F,F,F.

12
An Era of Economic Change

CHAPTER CHECKLIST

AGRICULTURE

Cotton, tobacco, corn and wheat. The important crops in the South.

Edmund Ruffin (1794-1865). A Virginia planter who introduced the use of marl, a soil rich in calcium, to counteract the acidity of worn-out tobacco fields. In 1832 he published an Essay on Calcareous Manures and he also edited the Farmers' Register (1833-1842). Ruffin's work in soil chemistry led to reforms in farming designed to rejuvenate southern agriculture.

SLAVERY

Isaac Franklin. An interstate slave trader who made a great deal of money in the 1850's. He and his partner, John Armfield, collected slaves in Alexandria, Virginia, and shipped them to a depot near Natchez. The business was so profitable that the prejudice against slave traders began to disappear. Franklin eventually retired and became a wealthy planter, owning six plantations in Louisiana and one in Tennessee.

Nat Turner. A slave who led a revolt in southern Virginia in 1831. The plot involved about 70 slaves, who killed 57 whites. In the counterattack that followed, 100 slaves were killed, and 20 more were executed following trial. The Nat Turner uprising was significant because the anxiety which it generated among whites led to stricter state laws governing slaves and free blacks alike, and a greater southern fear of the propaganda of the abolitionists.

Denmark Vesey. A West Indian slave who bought his freedom and settled in Charleston, South Carolina. For five years he plotted a slave uprising, but at the last minute his plans were betrayed to the authorities. The revelation of the conspiracy in 1822 led to arrests, trials, and 35 executions. It also resulted in a Negro Seaman's Act intended to prevent the entrance into Charleston of black sailors who might stir up unrest among South Carolina slaves.

MANUFACTURING

William Gregg. An important textile manufacturer in South Carolina, who established his factory at Graniteville in 1846. Gregg tried to weaken the general southern prejudice against manufacturing and business, and established a model community with schools and other facilities for the poor whites whom he hired as workers. By 1850 Gregg employed 300 white textile workers, a large number for the South but small when compared with northern manufacturers.

Industrial expansion. Factories were larger, more specialized, and more mechanized in the second quarter of the 19th century.

--Inventions were developed and workingmen quickly adapted to new machines.
--New natural resources were discovered and more raw materials such as cotton and grain were produced as settlement pushed west.
--Boilers and steam engines were developed and steampower began to replace water power.
--Immigration increased the labor supply.
--New sources of capital appeared as both Europeans and Americans invested in the economy, and California gold was added to the supply.
--Expanded markets brought about by transportation improvements, population growth, and the relatively high buying power of the people also contributed to the expansion of industry.

Labor.

--Irish and Germans made up most of the immigrant force, especially between 1847 and 1854. The Germans often moved into western farming areas whereas the Irish remained in urban centers, particularly working in New England mills.
--1840. Martin Van Buren granted the 10-hour day to federal employees.
--1842. Commonwealth v. Hunt, a Massachusetts court decision, established the basic legality of labor unions, but membership in unions before the Civil War remained small.

FOREIGN COMMERCE

Imports and exports. Cotton was the most valuable export;

textiles and iron products were the biggest imports. Most trade was with Great Britain.

sailing packet. A boat that follows a regular route, carrying passengers, freight, and mail. There were 52 packets operating between New York and various European ports by 1845, and more between New York and other coastal cities.

whaling fleets. Prospered between 1830 and 1860 and caused towns such as New Bedford, Massachusetts, to flourish. Whale oil was used in lanterns and for fuel.

clipper ships. Long, fast sailing ships which were built in Boston, New York, and Baltimore. They cut the sailing time from the Atlantic seaboard around South America to San Francisco from five or six months to three, but to achieve such speed, cargo capacity was sacrificed.

steamships. Captured much of the passenger and first-class freight movement by the late 1840's. Iron ships became more important and took away the advantage of American shipwrights and their cheap lumber supplies.

INTERNAL TRAVEL BY WATER

Mississippi River. Continued to move goods from farm to market, culminating in New Orleans.

Canals. Became increasingly important in the 1840's, particularly the Erie Canal, whose volume of western commerce continued to rise.

RAILROADS

1820's. First built in England, then in the United States.

Early problems.

--Different gauges, a gauge being the width between the two rails of the track. Companies varied the sizes deliberately to prevent other railroads from tying into their tracks.
--Engineering problems on curves and slopes.
--Fires caused by sparks from wood-burning locomotives.
--Weakness of wooden rails topped with strap iron.

Improvements.

--Engines that burned hard coal.
--Iron T-rail which improved the durability of the tracks.
--Crossties, that is, wood or metal beams which connected and supported the rails. They were a significant improvement because they reduced vibration.

1850's. A tremendous burst of railroad construction. See the map "Railroads 1850-1861" on pp. 328-329.

FINANCING RAILROADS

Private investors. Supplied three-fourths of capital before 1860. They generally preferred bonds to stocks. A stock is a certificate showing ownership of a portion of a corporation. The commitment can be short term for the stock can be sold at will. A bond is a certificate showing that a loan has been made to a corporation; no ownership is involved. The investor making the loan receives interest on his bond. The selling of both stocks and bonds were methods used to raise money for the railroads.

Public aid. Towns, counties, and states loaned money and invested in stocks. Some states granted exemption from taxation and the right to condemn property. Condemning property means that a governmental body forces a private owner to sell his property to that body for a public purpose. Some states actually built and operated railroads as public corporations. At the national level Congress did little because financial aid to railroads was usually blocked by a combination of eastern and southern votes.

"Land-grant" railroads. Railroads which received federal aid in the form of grants of public land. In 1850 Congress voted to give federal lands to the states to build a railroad from Lake Michigan to the Gulf of Mexico. The main beneficiary was the Illinois Central, which received a 200-foot right of way and alternate strips of land along the track one mile wide and six miles deep. The railroad company received a total of 2.6 million acres, and made money by mortgaging the land and selling portions to farmers. This method of aid was used extensively after the Civil War when the transcontinental railroad was being constructed.

Construction companies. Railroad capitalists were often more concerned with making money from constructing the lines than from operating them.

--Erastus Corning. An example of a railroad president who was also a banker and a manufacturer of iron. He accepted no salary as president of the Utica and Schenectady Railroad, but found it more profitable to sell the rails and other equipment to the company. Although Corning himself was honest, other railroad officials took personal advantage of similar deals.

OTHER TERMS TO IDENTIFY

Bright yellow. A new, mild variety of tobacco which was introduced in the early 1850's. It grew best in poor soil and gave a great stimulus to tobacco production.

1851, London Crystal Palace Exhibition. An exhibition of industrial products, inventions, and art objects housed in a huge glass structure. It was similar in concept to a present day world's fair. The American exhibit so impressed the British that they sent two special commissions to the United States to study manufacturing practices.

Elias Howe (1819-1867). A mechanic in a Lowell, Massachusetts, textile mill who invented the sewing machine. He received a patent in 1846, and its success made possible the readymade clothing industry.

John Deere (1804-1886). A blacksmith in Illinois who in 1839 began manufacturing steel plows rather than the earlier cast-iron models.

Cyrus Hall McCormick (1809-1884). Inventor of the reaper, a machine for harvesting grain, in 1831. In 1848 he located his factory at Chicago which was to become the transportation center for the farms of the Midwest. The McCormick reaper made possible a vast increase in grain output.

Panic of 1857. A temporary financial and agricultural set-back. An oversupply of grain on the world market caused grain prices to decline, which hurt railroads and their expansion, and this lessened the demand for other manufactured products. The economy rallied by 1859 but did not completely recover before the Civil War broke out.

GLOSSARY

bale. A large, compressed package of some product, such as cotton, which is bound together. The usual plantation cotton bale weighed 500 pounds.

barren. A tract of unproductive land, often covered with a scrubby growth of trees. "Poor white trash," a phrase used to describe white members of the lowest income group, scratched out a meager subsistence in the pine barrens of the Appalachian Mountains.

cheek by jowl. Jowl can mean either the cheek or the lower jaw. The term "cheek by jowl" means side by side or right next to each other. In the cities, tenements sprang up cheek by jowl with the expensive homes of the wealthy.

Deep South. The southeasternmost part of the United States, especially South Carolina, Georgia, Alabama, and Mississippi.

Emerald Isle. The island of Ireland. Many immigrants from the Emerald Isle came to the United States and settled in the large eastern seaports.

Freudian insight. Perception of a situation based on the theories of the Austrian physician, Sigmund Freud (1856-1939), developer of psychoanalysis. Freud emphasized the relationship between the subconscious and a person's actions.

manumission. Freeing from slavery, or emancipation. In 1859 in all the South only 3,000 blacks out of a slave population of nearly 4 million were manumitted.

proletarian class. Laborers, who work for a wage, not having enough capital, or money, to go into business for themselves or to invest in someone else's business. Karl Marx (1818-1883), the German philospher who is considered the founder of modern communism, referred to the working classes as the proletariat.

sell "down the river." The practice of selling slaves from the Upper South to buyers in the Deep South states because they brought a higher price. Today the term means to be exploited, to be taken advantage of.

status quo. An existing condition or the present state of affairs. The Latin term literally means "state in which." For example, most slaves in the pre-Civil War period did not question the status quo.

steerage. The section of a passenger ship, originally near the rudder, the steering apparatus. It provided the cheapest accomodations for passengers and was often used by immigrants coming to the United States. Note the picture on p. 320.

trunk line. The main line of a transportation or communication system. The number of trunk lines constructed by the railroads in the 1850's continued to grow, causing a decline in freight and passenger rates.

typhus. A serious disease characterized by severe headache, high fever, and a red rash. Epidemics of typhus often broke out among steerage passengers on ships crossing the Atlantic. For example, on one crossing of the ship Lark, 158 of 440 passengers died of typhus.

Upper South. The northern states of the South, such as Virginia, Maryland, and North Carolina. Tennessee and Kentucky are sometimes considered border states of the

Upper South.

windrow. A long row of cut hay or grain left to dry in a field before being bundled. McCormick's reaper deposited cut grain neatly on a platform from which a man could rake it easily into windrows.

DEFINE THE FOLLOWING, USING THE DICTIONARY IF NECESSARY

demise	seigneurial
euphemistically	unabated
paucity	vicissitudes
perforce	vulcanization
precipitous	warrens

SAMPLE QUESTIONS

MATCHING

1. ____	Edmund Ruffin	a.	slave trader.
2. ____	Isaac Franklin	b.	planned an abortive slave revolt in Charleston.
3. ____	Nat Turner	c.	invented sewing machine.
4. ____	Denmark Vesey	d.	textile manufacturer.
5. ____	William Gregg	e.	introduced marl to help tobacco fields.
6. ____	New Bedford	f.	developed the steel plow.
7. ____	Erastus Corning	g.	led slave insurrection in Virginia.
8. ____	John Deere	h.	manufactured reapers in Chicago.
9. ____	Elias Howe	i.	famous for whaling fleets.
10. ____	Cyrus McCormick	j.	railroad manager.

TRUE-FALSE

1. The largest number of immigrants in the 1850's came from Italy and France.

2. President Martin Van Buren granted the 8-hour day to federal employees in 1840.

3. Great Britain was the best customer of the United States and its leading supplier.

4. On the eve of the Civil War only one southern family in four owned any slaves.

5. Railroads and canals tied the West to the East more than to the South.

ANSWERS
MATCHING: e,a,g,b,d,i,j,f,c,h. TRUE-FALSE: F,F,T,T,T.

13

The Romantic Age

CHAPTER CHECKLIST

Romanticism. A 19th-century climate of opinion which emphasized feeling and intuition rather than thought and intellect. The importance of the individual and of nature was also stressed.

LITERATURE

Transcendentalism. A movement which emphasized an emotional, intuitive way of looking at life. Man and nature were all part of God, the combination of which was called the "Over-Soul."

Transcendentalist Club. An organization founded in Boston in 1836 which included among its members most of the New England literary establishment. The club was an informal discussion group, and its leading figure was Ralph Waldo Emerson.

Ralph Waldo Emerson (1803-1882). A transcendentalist writer who gave up his pulpit as a Unitarian minister to become an essayist and lecturer. He encouraged other writers to seek inspiration in their own surroundings rather than in European models, and thus develop a national American literature.

Henry David Thoreau (1817-1862). An individualist who was a member of the Transcendental Club. From 1845 to 1847 he lived at Walden Pond on Ralph Waldo Emerson's land, and used it as a retreat from civilization. In 1854 he published Walden which summarizes his individualistic philosophy and his love of nature. Later he became involved in the antislavery movement.

Edgar Allen Poe (1809-1849). A poet, critic, and short story writer who developed the detective story, as in "The Murders in the Rue Morgue," and was a master of the horror tale, such as "The Pit and the Pendulum." His most famous poem "The Raven" was published in 1845. Poe's personal life was chaotic. In 1849 he was found semiconscious in a Baltimore saloon and died four days later.

Nathaniel Hawthorne (1804-1864). A Massachusetts writer who drew heavily on the Puritan heritage of New England in his works. His novels dealt with the individual's struggle with sin and guilt. This theme could be seen in his most famous novels, The Scarlet Letter (1850) and House of the Seven Gables (1851).

Herman Melville (1819-1891). A novelist who spent his early life at sea and his later life writing fictionalized accounts of his travels. His most famous novel was Moby Dick published in 1851. Melville, like Hawthorne, had a dark view of human nature, unlike the optimistic idealism of the transcendentalists.

Walt Whitman (1819-1892). A poet whose most famous work was a collection of poems entitled Leaves of Grass. The first edition came out in 1848 and contained 12 poems. Whitman continued to add to the volume, and in 1860 Leaves of Grass had grown to 122 poems. The ninth and final edition appeared in 1892, the year of Whitman's death.

POPULAR READING

penny newspapers. Cheap newsheets which depended on sensation, crime stories, and society gossip to appeal to the masses. The first was the New York Sun which came out in 1833.

"domestic" novels. Moralistic, sentimental stories whose themes were similar to today's soap operas.

religious books. The American Tract Society was a group which published and distributed religious tracts. A tract is a pamphlet or booklet which makes a declaration or appeal, usually a religious or political one. The society did not promote the doctrines of any particular Christian denomination, but sent out missionary-salesmen to preach the gospel and sell or give away religious books. The American Bible Society had similar goals and issued hundreds of thousands of copies of the Old and New Testaments of the Bible each year.

CULTURE

Education.

lyceums. Mutual improvement societies which might be compared to today's adult continuing education programs. The first lyceum was started in Massachusetts in 1826 by Josiah Holbrook. Soon there were thousands of these lecture and discussion clubs all over the United States, co-ordinated by the National American Lyceum.

Architecture.

American Gothic. A style of architecture popular in the 19th century which often included towers, steeples, arches, and elaborate wood trim. Note the picture on p. 348. It was a scaled-down adaptation of Gothic architecture which was used in western Europe from the 12th through the 15th centuries.

Art.

genre painters. Artists whose paintings depicted scenes and subjects of everyday life. Their work was designed to appeal to the general public. See the picture by William Sidney Mount on p. 349.

Hudson River school. A group of artists who created large landscape paintings of America's countryside, particularly of the Hudson River valley in New York. About a dozen painters comprised the group, and their canvases reflected the same concern with nature that the transcendentalists expressed in literature.

Currier and Ives. Print makers who specialized in lithographs depicting American life, manners, and history. The firm operated by Nathaniel Currier (1813-1888) and James Merritt Ives (1824-1895) sold cheap prints in quantity, and from the 1850's brought this form of art into many American homes.

REFORM MOVEMENTS

Religion.

Rappites. Followers of the religious leader George Rapp (1757-1847), who left Germany with 600 people and founded a religious community in 1804 near Pittsburgh. The Rappites believed the millennium, or the second coming of Jesus followed by the end of the world, was about to take place. Therefore, everyone should be prepared. The group worked their land communally, shared the produce, and practiced celibacy.

Shakers. Members of a religious movement founded by Ann Lee (1736-1784), who by the 1830's had established about 20 communities where they could practice their beliefs. Like the Rappites, the Shakers held property in common, practiced celibacy, and believed the millennium was imminent. The official name of the sect was the United Society of Believers in Christ's Second Coming. They got the name Shaker from their early custom of dancing with shaking movements during ceremonies.

Mormons. Members of a new religion founded by Joseph Smith

in the 1820's, officially named the Church of Jesus Christ of Latter Day Saints. The Mormons had a flourishing settlement in Nauvoo, Illinois, from 1839, but then in 1847, because of the resentment of their neighbors, they moved west to Utah under the leadership of Brigham Young. Characteristics of the early church were a strong sense of community cooperation and the practice of polygamy, that is, the men could have more than one wife.

Prison.

Philadelphia System. A prison system based on strict solitary confinement so that a prisoner could reflect on his wrongdoings and hopefully reform his ways.

Auburn System. A prison system developed in New York State which allowed some social contact and work in shops and stone quarries. Absolute silence was required and whippings were administered for the slightest breaking of the rules.

Mental Hospitals.

Dorothea Dix (1802-1887). A reformer who persuaded the Massachusetts legislature and then other states to improve the care of the mentally ill. In her surveys she found that people with mental problems were often held in prisons and jails, and her efforts were instrumental in the establishment of 32 state mental hospitals.

Temperance.

American Temperance Union. Founded in 1826, the Union started a crusade to get people to "sign the pledge" not to drink alcoholic beverages. The word temperance usually means moderation, but the Temperance Union wanted people to abstain completely from drinking liquor. Another goal was to prohibit by law the sale of alcoholic beverages, and in 1846 Maine became the first state to pass such legislation. The prohibition movement culminated in 1919 with the passage of the 18th Amendment to the Constitution prohibiting the sale of liquor. This amendment was reversed in 1933 with the 21st Amendment.

Abolition.

William Lloyd Garrison (1805-1879). A leader of the abolitionist movement who called for an immediate rather than a gradual end to slavery. Garrison established a newspaper, The Liberator (1831-1865), to spread his message and founded several anti-slavery societies. He was considered one of the most radical and uncompromising of the abolitionists.

Theodore Dwight Weld (1803-1895). A minister dedicated to the emancipation, or freeing, of slaves. He was willing to accept a more gradual approach than Garrison. Weld used an emotional appeal and was active in the abolitionist movement in the 1830's.

Frederick Douglass (1817-1895). A slave who escaped to the North and became an abolitionist leader. He gave anti-slavery lectures in the United States and Great Britain, wrote a moving autobiography, Narrative of the Life of Frederick Douglass (1845), and in 1847 founded The North Star, an abolitionist newspaper. Douglass and Weld were willing to work within the governmental structure to obtain change, whereas Garrison once burned a copy of the Constitution to show his disdain for a system which allowed slavery.

Underground railroad. The system used to help escaped slaves flee the South and reach a northern free state or Canada. "Conductors" were the persons who hid the slaves along the way. Note the advertisement on p. 361.

1842, Prigg v. Pennsylvania. A Supreme Court decision which said that the states did not have to enforce the federal Fugitive Slave Law. As a result, some northern states passed "personal liberty" laws barring state officials from aiding in the capture and return of runaway slaves. Southern resentment against these acts led to the stricter Fugitive Slave Law included in the Compromise of 1850.

1836-1844, "gag rule." A measure passed in the House of Representatives at the insistence of southern congressmen. It required that all petitions sent to the House requesting anti-slavery action be laid on the table, that is, ignored. This action was particularly designed to stop routine petitions urging the abolition of the slave trade in Washington, D.C. Former president John Quincy Adams, now representative from Massachusetts, was an outspoken opponent of the "gag rule," claiming that it violated the right to petition the Government guaranteed in the First Amendment.

Women's Rights.

Elizabeth Cady Stanton (1815-1892). An abolitionist who turned to women's rights when she attended the World Anti-Slavery Convention in London in 1840 and found that women were not allowed to participate in the debates. She helped organize the Seneca Falls Convention in 1848, and in 1869 was elected president of the National Woman Suffrage Association, an office she held for 21 years. The suffrage movement campaigned for women's right to vote, and it was eventually successful at the national level in 1920 with the 19th Amendment.

1848, Seneca Falls Convention. A meeting in Seneca Falls, New York, which began the women's rights movement in the United States. It was organized by Elizabeth Cady Stanton and Lucretia Mott and about 300 persons, including 40 men, gathered to hear a Declaration of Principles based on the Declaration of Independence.

Susan B. Anthony (1820-1906). A reformer who was primarily known as a campaigner for women's rights, although she was also active in abolitionist and temperance societies. She was a close associate of Elizabeth Cady Stanton in the suffrage movement.

OTHER TERMS TO IDENTIFY

Henry Wadsworth Longfellow (1807-1882). A poet and professor of modern languages at Harvard who was famous for such poems as "The Village Blacksmith," "Paul Revere's Ride," and The Song of Hiawatha.

James Russell Lowell (1819-1891). A poet and literary critic who succeeded Longfellow as professor of modern languages at Harvard. Lowell became the first editor of the Atlantic Monthly, founded in Boston in 1857.

George Bancroft (1800-1891). An historian who is sometimes called the "father of American history" because of his ten-volume History of the United States which came out between 1834 and 1874. Bancroft was also secretary of the navy, acting secretary of the army, and ambassador to Great Britain and to Germany.

William Hickling Prescott (1796-1859). An historian who wrote extensively on Spain and her empire in America. His most famous works were Conquest of Mexico (1843) and Conquest of Peru (1847).

Francis Parkman (1823-1893). An historian who wrote about the struggle between France and Great Britain for the control of North America.

William Gilmore Simms (1806-1870). A Southern writer of the romantic era whose favorite theme was the South Carolina frontier. Simms' works, along with those of another southern writer, John Pendleton Kennedy, contributed much to the glamorous legend of the Old South.

Horace Mann (1796-1859). A pioneer in the reform of public education. He was the first secretary of the Massachusetts Board of Education (1837-1848), and urged such reforms as a minimum school year of six months and professional teacher training.

Brook Farm. A utopian community in Massachusetts which existed from 1841 to 1847. Its founder was George Ripley and the settlement became a retreat for transcendentalists. The farm was a communal society in which labor was shared.

Charles Fourier (1772-1837). A French utopian socialist who believed that the natural inclinations of man, if properly channeled, would result in social harmony. Society should be organized into phalanxes, an economic unit composed of 1,620 people. Persons would live in a community building and divide the work among them. In the 1840's several dozen Fourierist colonies were established in the United States; none lasted very long.

GLOSSARY

Antichrist. The great antagonist or enemy who was expected by Christians to set himself up against Christ and fill the world with wickedness in the last days before Jesus Christ's Second Coming. The anti-Roman Catholic movement in this country, sponsored by Protestant Christians, viewed the Pope, the head of the Roman Catholic Church, as being the Antichrist, a tyrant seeking to overcome the United States.

atheism. Disbelief or denial of the existence of God. Robert Owen, the British utopian socialist who bought the Rappite settlement at New Harmony, Indiana, advocated what he called "enlightened atheism," a point which made him unpopular with the religious majority in nearby communities.

chauvinist. One who is militant or boastful concerning a particular cause. The term was named after Nicholas Chauvin, a French solider who was extremely devoted to Napoleon. Today the term male chauvinist is used to refer to a man who tries to bolster the importance of the male sex by putting down or ridiculing women.

communitarian. A member or supporter of a community in which there are no social classes and in which there is common ownership of the means of production. The Rappites and the Shakers were examples of communitarians.

gentile. One who is not of the Jewish faith, particularly a Christian as distinguished from a Jew. Among Mormons, however, a gentile is any person who is not a Mormon.

phrenology. The practice of studying a person's character and mental capabilities from the contours of the head. Different segments of the head supposedly controlled such characteristics as self-esteem, friendship, and hope.

pirate. To reproduce the literary works of an author without permission. The works of English novelists were frequently pirated by American publishers.

printer's devil. An apprentice in a printing establishment. At age 13 Walt Whitman left school and became a printer's devil.

prognathous. Having jaws that project forward to a considerable degree. One writer of the early 19th century claimed that the Negro belonged to the "prognathous" species of man, meaning that he was similar to early, prehistoric man. The same author said the black had a nervous system "somewhat like the ourangoutang," a type of ape whose name today is generally spelled orangutan. These ideas illustrate the pseudo-scientific language used in the pre-Civil War period to try to prove the Negro was racially inferior.

Smithsonian Institute. The national museum in Washington, D.C., founded in 1846. It was named after James Smithson (1765-1829), a British chemist and mineralogist who left a bequest to found such an institution. The original museum is in the American Gothic style, but the new addition completed in the 1960's is more modern in style. The Smithsonian is often referred to as "the nation's attic."

"whore of Babylon." A reference to Revelation 17: 5 in the Bible, wherein the ancient city of Babylon is called "the mother of whores and of every obscenity on earth." Protestant groups sometimes referred to the Roman Catholic Church as "the whore of Babylon."

zealot. Person who is fanatically committed to a cause. George Rapp was a religious zealot who moved with many of his followers from Germany to the United States.

Zion. A place or community regarded as being especially devoted to God. The Mormons established their Zion on the shores of the Great Salt Lake in Utah.

DEFINE THE FOLLOWING, USING THE DICTIONARY IF NECESSARY

allegorical
axiomatic
charlatan
cloying
ethereal
mountebank
omnivorously
pernicious
prodigality
ratiocination

SAMPLE QUESTIONS

MATCHING

1. ___	Elizabeth Cady Stanton	a.	novelist who wrote Moby Dick.
2. ___	William Lloyd Garrison	b.	leader of the Mormons when they moved to Utah.
3. ___	Dorothea Dix	c.	leading figure of the Transcendental Club in Boston.

4. ___Frederick Douglass
5. ___Ann Lee
6. ___Joseph Smith
7. ___Herman Melville
8. ___ Edgar Allen Poe
9. ___ Brigham Young
10. ___ Henry David Thoreau

d. a slave who became an abolitionist leader.
e. a reformer who improved conditions for the mentally ill.
f. the transcendentalist author of <u>Walden</u>.
g. an abolitionist leader who edited <u>The Liberator</u>.
h. a crusader for women's rights who organized the Seneca Falls Convention in 1848.
i. a writer who often used detective, science-fiction, and horror themes.
j. founder of the Mormon Church.
k. founder of the Shakers.

TRUE-FALSE

1. Currier and Ives founded a religious settlement in New Harmony, Indiana.
2. Hudson River school was a form of popular education in which people attended a lecture series.
3. Philadelphia System was a prison system based on solitary confinement.
4. The Temperance Union encouraged persons to sign a pledge to drink alcoholic beverages only in moderation.
5. The gag rule was designed to cut off debate on woman's suffrage.

ANSWERS
MATCHING: h,g,e,d,k,j,a,i,b,f. TRUE-FALSE: F,F,T,F,F.

14

The Coming of the Civil War

CHAPTER CHECKLIST

STEPS LEADING TO WAR

Uncle Tom's Cabin. Harriet Beecher Stowe's novel which heightened antislavery sentiment around the world. Mrs. Stowe began writing it while debate raged over the Fugitive Slave Act of 1850, and it first appeared in serial form in the National Era, an antislavery periodical, from June, 1851, to April, 1852. The book was also successfully adapted as a play, and the characters of the slaves Uncle Tom and Eliza, the white child Eva, and the slave driver Simon Legree became well known.

"Young America" movement. An expansionist feeling which attempted to project the spirit of manifest destiny south to Latin America, west into the Pacific Islands, and north to Canada. This climate of opinion was evident in the late 1840's and 1850's, and exhibited a desire to spread American democracy to other areas.

1854, Ostend Manifesto. A secret report on Cuba prepared in Ostend, Belgium, by three American diplomats in Europe: James Buchanan, minister to Great Britain, John Mason, minister to France, and Pierre Soulé, minister to Spain. The report was sent to Secretary of State William Marcy and outlined the rationale for buying, or if necessary, taking the island of Cuba from Spain. The news leaked out, and northerners were convinced it was a southern plot to acquire another slave state. The publicity wrecked any hope of obtaining Cuba.

FRANKLIN PIERCE (1804-1869), 14th President

--Born in New Hampshire.
--Democratic member of the House of Representatives.
--United States Senator from New Hampshire.
--President (1853-1857).

1853, Gadsden Purchase. A treaty with Mexico negotiated by the United States minister James Gadsden. For $10 million the United States acquired land in present-day New Mexico and Arizona which included an easy route over the mountains for a railroad. This purchase made possible a southern route for the proposed transcontinental railroad.

1854, Kansas-Nebraska Act. Legislation sponsored by Senator Stephen Douglas which officially created the Nebraska Territory and the Kansas Territory. In addition, it repealed the 1820 Missouri Compromise and stated that popular sovereignty would determine the future of slavery in those two areas, rather than the previous dividing line of 36° 30'. The act reopened the issue of the extension of slavery into the territories, and caused further difficulties between the North and the South.

New political parties.

--Know-Nothing Party. Also known as the American party, active between 1853 and 1856. It was anti-Roman Catholic and anti-immigrant. The party got its name because originally it was a secret organization for Protestants whose password was "I don't know." Calling themselves the American party in 1856, they ran Millard Fillmore for president. By this time, however, the party was split over the slavery issue, and many northern supporters joined the Republicans.

--Republican Party. Started in 1854, composed of former Free-Soilers, Conscience Whigs (the Whigs who opposed slavery), "Anti-Nebraska" Democrats (opposed the Kansas-Nebraska Act), and northern members of the Know-Nothings. The one major demand of the party was that slavery be kept out of the territories, but they did not propose abolishing it where it already was. This party, started in the 1850's, is the same Republican party in existence today. It should not be confused with Jefferson's Democratic-Republican party which is today's Democratic party.

Bleeding Kansas. A term referring to the violence in the Kansas Territory as pro-slavery and anti-slavery forces tried to take hold in the area after it was opened as a territory in 1854.

1856, Caning of Charles Sumner (1811-1874). An event which illustrated the emotional response of southerners to abolitionists. Charles Sumner, senator from Massachusetts from 1851 until 1874, made an impassioned speech in the Senate against the Kansas situation and slavery in general, and in the speech he made insulting remarks about a southern colleague and slaveowner, Senator Andrew Butler of South Carolina, who was not present. Two days later Butler's nephew, Preston Brooks, a member of the House of Representatives from South Carolina, marched over to the Senate to redeem the family honor. Brooks waited until the Senate adjourned and then went down to Sumner, still writing at his desk, and beat him with his walking cane. Primarily because of psychological damage, Sumner was unable to return to the Senate for three years. Brooks was officially censured, or reprimanded, by the House of Representatives for his actions, so he resigned his seat and was then triumphantly reelected by his South Carolina constituents.

JAMES BUCHANAN (1791-1868), 15th President

--Born in Pennsylvania, worked as an attorney.
--Began his political career as a Federalist but switched to the Democratic Party in the 1820's.
--Member of the House of Representatives from Pennsylvania.
--Minister to Russia.
--United States Senator.
--Secretary of State under President Polk (1845-1849).
--Minister to Great Britain (1853-1856).
--President (1857-1861).

1857, Dred Scott decision. The Supreme Court stated that Congress could not deny a person the right to take his property, including slaves, into any territory he wished. Dred Scott was a slave who was taken by his master, an army surgeon, from Missouri, a slave state, into Illinois, a free state, and then Wisconsin, a territory declared free under the Missouri Compromise. Scott then returned to Missouri, and after his master died, he sued for freedom on the grounds that residency in free areas had made him free. Scott's emancipation was not really in question because his master's widow had married an abolitionist, and Scott was to be freed no matter what the outcome. The Supreme Court, presided over by Chief Justice Roger Taney, made several pronouncements in this decision. First, it declared that a slave was not a citizen and therefore could not sue in a federal court. Furthermore, under the Constitution, the government could not deprive a person of life, liberty, or property without due process of law, and therefore the 1820 Missouri Compromise, even before it had been repealed by the 1854 Kansas-Nebraska Act, had been unconstitutional. In summary, the Dred Scott decision declared a law of Congress unconstitutional for the first time since Marbury v. Madison (1803). It also stated that slavery could not be excluded from federal territories.

1856, Lecompton Constitution. A proslavery document drawn up at a constitutional convention in Lecompton, Kansas. The freesoil forces refused to participate in the election of delegates to this convention. President Buchanan encouraged Congress to accept the proposed state constitution and to admit Kansas as a slave state, but the opposition, led by Stephen Douglas, was able to prevent it. Two separate referendums were held in Kansas in 1858 to decide whether or not to accept the Lecompton Constitution. In both cases, the document was rejected. Kansas finally entered the Union in 1861 as a free state.

1858, Lincoln-Douglas debates. Held in Illinois where the Republican, Abraham Lincoln, and the Democrat, Stephen Douglas, were competing for a seat in the United States Senate. Since senators were elected by the state legislatures until the 17th Amendment passed in 1913, the two men were not appealing directly to the people for votes, but were asking them to elect certain state legislators who would in turn vote for them for senator. One major issue was whether or not slavery should be excluded from the territories. Douglas won the election but Lincoln won national recognition as a spokesman for Republican principles.

--Freeport Doctrine. A point made by Douglas at the debate held in Freeport, Illinois, which illustrated his continued support for popular sovereignty. Lincoln asked Douglas if, considering the Dred Scott decision, a territory could exclude slavery. The Supreme Court had said it could not, but Douglas replied that if local police officials did not enforce slavery regulations, then the institution would not exist. In other words it would be difficult for slavery to exist in an area where the local populace did not want it. This pronouncement hurt Douglas two years later when he was the Democratic presidental candidate because southern Democrats refused to accept a man who said the Dred Scott decision could be circumvented.

1859, John Brown's Raid. An attack on a United States arsenal at Harper's Ferry, Virginia, led by John Brown, an ardent abolitionist who was mentally unbalanced. With 16 white and 5 black men he made his raid, planning to distribute the weapons captured to local slaves who would join the uprising. Brown was tried and hanged, and he became a martyr to northern abolitionists.

Election of 1860. Lincoln won the election in which four parties nominated candidates. Note the map entitled "The Election of 1860" on p. 391.

--Republican. Lincoln led the Republicans in opposing the extension of slavery into the territories.
--Democratic. Stephen Douglas got the support of the northern Democrats but his Freeport Doctrine caused southerners to bolt the party.
--Democratic. John C. Breckinridge of Kentucky was the nominee of the southern Democrats, who declared that citizens could take their "property" into any territory.
--Constitutional Union. John Bell of Tennessee led those remnants of Whigs and Know-Nothings who tried to ignore the slavery issue.

December 20, 1860. A special convention called by the South Carolina legislature voted to secede from the Union. Within six weeks they were joined by the other states of the Lower South.

February, 1861. In Montgomery, Alabama a provisional government of the Confederate States of America was established. It was later moved to Richmond. Jefferson Davis was elected president.

OTHER TERMS TO IDENTIFY

William Walker (1824-1860). An American filibuster who seized control of Nicaragua and made himself president for two years from 1855 to 1857. There were even rumors concerning communication with President Pierce about the admission of Nicaragua as a slave state. In 1860, while trying to recapture part of Central America, Walker was captured and shot in Honduras.

"General" George W.L. Bickley. An adventurer who tried to organize an expedition into northern Mexico. He attempted to get the support of proslavery factions by suggesting that Mexico be divided into no less than 25 slave states.

1850, Clayton-Bulwer Treaty. Negotiated by Secretary of State John Clayton and the British minister Sir Henry Bulwer, the treaty provided that any future canal built across Central America would be jointly controlled by the two countries. This treaty governed Anglo-American relations in the area until the 1901 Hay-Pauncefote Treaty which gave the United States the right to construct and own such a canal by herself.

Stephen Douglas (1813-1861). Democratic Illinois senator, known as the "Little Giant," who was an advocate of popular sovereignty in the territories. He helped steer the Compromise of 1850, and sponsored the Kansas-Nebraska Act of 1854. In 1860 he was the presidential candidate for the northern wing of the Democratic Party. Douglas died suddenly from typhoid fever in 1861.

New England Emigrant Aid Society. An organization formed in 1854 to help antislavery settlers move to Kansas. Their goal was to assure that when the time came for popular sovereignty to decide whether Kansas would enter the Union as a free or a slave state, the area would have a majority of antislavery forces.

Border Ruffians. Men from Missouri who crossed the border into Kansas to vote illegally, primarily for proslavery candidates. In 1854 they were partially responsible for electing a proslavery territorial delegate to Congress, and in 1855 the Border Ruffians helped elect a proslavery territorial legislature.

John C. Frémont (1813-1890). An explorer known as "the Pathfinder" and a hero of the conquest of California during the Mexican War. Frémont was the first Republican candidate for President in 1856, and the party slogan that year was "Free soil, free speech, and Frémont." Frémont lost to the Democrat, James Buchanan.

1861, Crittenden Compromise. A constitutional amendment proposed by Senator John J. Crittenden of Kentucky and a group of moderates. They proposed that slavery be authorized in all territories south of latitude 36° 30', the old Missouri Compromise line, and that no future amendment would tamper with the institution of slavery where it already existed. Lincoln and his Republican supporters refused to consider opening any new territory to slavery, and the attempted compromise died.

GLOSSARY

buttonhole. A slit in a garment for fastening a button, but also a figure of speech meaning to detain someone. In other words, grabbing a person by his buttonholes is a way of making him listen to what you have to say. Before the 1852 nominating convention, Stephen Douglas toured the country, buttonholing the local bigwigs of the Democratic Party.

Capitol. The building in Washington, D.C., which houses the Congress of the United States. The capital is the town or city that is the official seat of government in a state or nation.

crepe. A fabric which worn or displayed in black is a sign of mourning. When Anthony Burns, a runaway slave from Virginia was arrested in Boston, a sympathetic mob tried to free him. The federal commissioner finally ruled that he must be returned to his master, and as he and a military escort marched to the dock to board a ship, buildings all along the route were festooned, or draped, with black crepe, as a sign of mourning for returning the fugitive slave.

guttapercha cane. A walking stick made from the latex of a guttapercha tree, a tropical tree most commonly found in Malaysia. The texture of the substance resembles rubber.

Lower South. A term used to refer to the states of South Carolina, Georgia, Florida, Alabama, Mississippi, Louisiana, and Texas. The states of the Lower South had seceded by February 1, 1861.

Mason-Dixon line. The boundary between Pennsylvania and Maryland as surveyed by Charles Mason and Jeremiah Dixon between 1763 and 1767. It was regarded as the division between the free and the slave states before the Civil War.

wheelhorse. A steady, dependable worker, especially in a political organization. Abraham Lincoln was a party wheelhorse, first as a Whig, then as a Republican. In a team of horses, the wheelhorse is the horse that follows the leader and is harnessed nearest to the front wheels.

writ of habeas corpus. A document which states that a person is to be brought before a court or judge, so that the person may be released if held unlawfully. When a newspaperman in Wisconsin was arrested for rousing a mob to free a captured runaway slave, the state court released him on a writ of habeas corpus.

DEFINE THE FOLLOWING, USING THE DICTIONARY IF NECESSARY

cacophony
congenitally
fallacious
importuned
megalomaniac
moribund
pique
punctilio
quixotic
reneging

SAMPLE QUESTIONS

MULTIPLE CHOICE

1. The Ostend Manifesto concerned the possible annexation of:
   a. Hawaii.
   b. Cuba.
   c. Nicaragua.
   d. Mexico.

2. The status of slavery in the territory of the Lousiana Purchase was not affected by the:
   a. Dred Scott decision.
   b. Kansas-Nebraska Act.
   c. Compromise of 1850.
   d. Missouri Compromise.

3. Which was a provision of the Kansas-Nebraska Act?
   a. Kansas was declared a free state.
   b. the Dred Scott decision was nullified.
   c. popular sovereignty was provided for in these two territories.
   d. the 36° 30' line was extended to the Pacific.

4. The original platform of the Republican Party:
   a. abolition of slavery.
   b. popular sovereignty in the territories.
   c. no expansion of slavery into the territories.
   d. ignore the issue of slavery.

5. What was the principal established by the Dred Scott decision?
   a. Congress could abolish slavery in the territories at will.
   b. slaves residing in a free state automatically became free.
   c. the status of slaves could not be changed by national legislation.
   d. through popular sovereignty, the territories had the sole right to determine the status of slavery.

TRUE-FALSE

1. The activities of William Walker in Nicaragua reflected the spirit of the Young America movement of the 1850's.

2. The Gadsden Purchase was desired as a haven for freed slaves.

3. The Lecompton Constitution was supported by the pro-slavery faction in Kansas.

4. The Freeport Doctrine stated that even though slavery was legal in territories, it could not exist where local officials did not enforce it.

5. The first southern state to secede from the Union was Alabama.

ANSWERS
MULTIPLE CHOICE: b,c,c,c. TRUE-FALSE: T,F,T,F.

15

The War to Save the Union

CHAPTER CHECKLIST

ABRAHAM LINCOLN (1809-1865), 16th President --Born in Kentucky, grew up in Indiana and Illinois. --Practiced law and served in the Illinois legislature as a Whig for eight years. --Member of the House of Representatives (1847-1849). --Ran for the United States Senate in 1858 as a Republican, defeated by Stephen Douglas. --President (1861-1865). --Assassinated on April 12, 1865, by John Wilkes Booth in Washington, D.C.

Jefferson Davis (1808-1889).

--Born in Kentucky, grew up in Mississippi, educated at West Point.
--Democratic member of the House of Representatives (1845-1846) and of the Senate (1847-1851).
--Secretary of War under President Pierce (1853-1857).
--President of the Confederate States of America (1861-1865).
--Imprisoned for two years after the Civil War, but released without being tried for treason.

THE UNION SPLITS

December 20, 1860. South Carolina seceded from the Union and was soon followed by Mississippi (January 9, 1861), Florida (January 10), Alabama (January 11), Georgia (January 19), Louisiana (January 26), and Texas (February 1).

April 12, 1861. First shots of the war fired at Fort Sumter, South Carolina. Lincoln issued a call for volunteers.

April-May, 1861. Other states seceded: Virginia (April 17), Arkansas (May 6), Tennessee (May 7), and North Carolina (May 20).

Advantages of each side.

--North had seven times as much manufacturing and a far larger and more efficient railroad system. The North also controlled the merchant marine and the navy with which to blockade the southern states. Furthermore, it had a larger population.

--South thought Europe needed southern cotton and predicted, **incorrectly,** that European countries, particularly Great Britain, would come to her aid. The South fought a defensive war, which was cheaper in terms of men and material and maintained morale. Southerners fought to defend their homes as well as to protect the institution of slavery. Most important, the South had superior military leadership.

OUTSTANDING GENERALS

North.

Ulysses Simpson Grant (1822-1885). A West Point graduate who fought in the Mexican War and resigned from the army in 1854. He held a series of jobs and had bouts with alcoholism, but when the Civil War broke out he reenlisted and quickly rose in rank. His most important victories were at Vicksburg and at Appomattox. Grant later became Republican president from 1869 to 1877.

George McClellan (1826-1885). A West Point graduate who became general in chief of the army in 1861, was removed from that position the following year, reinstated and removed once again, all in 1862. Lincoln's chief complaint against McClellan was that he dallied rather than pursuing the enemy. He was the unsuccessful Democratic candidate for president in 1864, and after the war he pursued an engineering career and served as governor of New Jersey (1878-1881).

William Tecumseh Sherman (1820-1891). Like Grant and McClellan, a West Point graduate who resigned from the army in the 1850's and reenlisted at the beginning of the Civil War. His most famous campaign was in Georgia in 1864 and is referred to as Sherman's "march to the sea." Sherman is sometimes called "the first modern soldier" because he believed in total war, that is, in appropriating or destroying everything that might help the enemy continue the fight. After the war Sherman served as general in chief of the army for 14 years.

South.

Robert Edward Lee (1807-1870). A Virginian who graduated from West Point and followed a military career. In 1862 he became commander of Confederate forces and is generally considered the best overall strategist of the war. In 1865 Lee surrendered his Army of Northern Virginia to Grant at Appomattox Court House. After the war he became president of Washington College in Virginia, now called Washington and Lee University.

Thomas J. (Stonewall) Jackson, (1824-1863). A Virginian, educated at West Point, who served six years in the army and then resigned to teach. As a general for the Confederacy, he won his nickname at the First Battle of Bull Run in 1861, when a fellow officer trying to rally his own men shouted, "Look, there is Jackson with his Virginians, standing like a stone wall against the enemy." Jackson was particularly noted for the swift striking capacity of his troops. His last battle was at Chancellorsville in 1863 where he was accidentally shot and killed by his own troops.

MAJOR BATTLES

1861, Fort Sumter, South Carolina. The first shots of the war were fired on this Union fortress on an island in the Charleston harbor. By April the Union troops there needed food, and Lincoln ordered supply ships to go to the island. The Confederates opened fire before the ships arrived and the next day the fort fell into southern hands.

July, 1861, Bull Run, Virginia. A battle fought on a branch of the Potomac River called Bull Run, which the Confederates won. It is also called the Battle of Manassas, after a nearby town. General McDowell was the Union commander and General Beauregard led the Confederate troops. As a result of this battle the Union troops retreated in panic to Washington, D.C., 20 miles away, and many people thought the capital would fall next.

There was a Second Battle of Bull Run in August, 1862, in which Lee's army was victorious over the Union troops led by General John Pope.

April, 1862, Shiloh, Tennessee. A Union victory led by General Grant over the Confederate forces of General Albert Sidney Johnston. Shiloh was a country church 20 miles north of Corinth, Mississippi. Johnston led a suprise attack on Grant's troops and was successful until fresh Union troops were brought in and the southerners fell back. But Grant had been caught off guard and was temporarily relieved of his command. Note the map "War in the West, 1862" on p. 409.

September, 1862, Antietam Creek, Maryland. A battle at Sharpsburg led by General McClellan against the Confederate troops of General Lee. Lee had hoped for a victory in a non-Confederate state but he was outnumbered and his troops were able to slip back into Virginia only because McClellan did not aggressively pursue his advantage. As a result of the Battle of Antietam, Lincoln dismissed McClellan from his command. Note the map "Lee's Antietam Campaign 1862" on p. 412.

<u>July, 1863, Gettysburg, Pennsylvania</u>. The turning point in the Civil War where General Lee's troops were clearly defeated on the battlefield by the Union forces under General George Meade. However, Meade did not continue his attack and Lee's army retreated to safety in Virginia. Note the map "Gettysburg Campaign 1863" on p. 419.

<u>May-July, 1863, Vicksburg, Mississippi</u>. General Grant placed the city, defended by General John C. Pemberton, under siege and starved it into submission. The city was important because of its commanding position on the Mississippi River. With Vicksburg in Union hands, federal gunboats could range up and down on the river, and Arkansas and Texas, the breadbasket of the Confederacy, were isolated. Note the map "Grant's Vicksburg Campaign 1863" on p. 422.

<u>September-December, 1864, March through Georgia</u>. General Sherman took Atlanta and then marched his army to the port of Savannah. The troops were permitted to live off the land, and as they marched, they denuded a strip of Georgia 60 miles wide. This display of the North's determination to carry the fight to a conclusion broke the South's will. Note the map "Sherman's Campaigns 1864-1865" on p. 426.

<u>April 3, 1865, Richmond, Virginia</u>. The Confederate capital fell to Grant's army.

<u>April 9, 1865, Appomattox Court House, Virginia</u>. General Lee surrendered his army to General Grant at a prearranged ceremony in a house in this village. The requirement was that the Confederate soldiers lay down their arms and they could return to their homes in peace. They were also allowed to retain possession of their horses.

IMPORTANT ACTS DURING THE WAR

<u>Conscription</u>. When the number of volunteers began to slacken, both sides instituted a draft.

--South, 1862, Conscription Act. The draft act passed by the Confederate Congress. It allowed the hiring of substitutes and exempted many classes of people, including college professors and mail carriers. There was also a provision deferring the owners of 20 or more slaves.

--North, 1863, Conscription Act. Applied to all men between 20 and 45, but it allowed draftees to hire substitutes and even to buy exemption for $300. Many workingmen resented this discrimination against the poor, and draft riots broke out in various parts of the nation, the most serious occurring in New York City. Note the picture on p. 417.

1862, Emancipation Proclamation. Issued by Lincoln on September 22 to go into effect on January 1, 1863. It stated that all slaves in areas of rebellion on that date would be free. The Proclamation did not apply to the border states or to areas of the South which had already been captured by federal troops. However, as Union troops moved into new areas of the Confederacy, those slaves would be freed. Actually, all slaves were not freed until the ratification of the Thirteenth Amendment to the Constitution in 1865.

1862, Homestead Act. Gave 160 acres of public land to any settler who would farm the land for five years.

1862, Morrill Land Grant Act. Gave the states land at the rate of 30,000 acres for each Representative and Senator from that state to support agricultural colleges. Some states gave the land to existing schools while others founded new institutions. About 70 new colleges were started as a result.

1862, Pacific Railway Act. Authorized subsidies in land and money for the construction of a transcontinental railroad which was completed in 1869. This act had been delayed for a decade as the North and South fought over the route. With the southern states no longer represented in Congress, the selection of a route was more easily made.

1863, National Banking Act. Banks would obtain federal charters by investing at least one-third of their capital in United States bonds, and then issuing currency up to 90 per cent of the value of these bonds. In addition a 10 per cent tax was placed on state bank notes issued. This act eventually drove the state notes out of circulation, and established a uniform national currency as we have today.

RESULTS OF THE WAR

--Negro slavery was dead.
--The Union could not be dissolved; secession was not possible.
--A republican form of government could survive, despite the dissatisfaction of a minority.
--Inventions, technical advancements, and a better organized, more productive economic system had emerged.

OTHER TERMS TO IDENTIFY

"Iron-back" Republicans. Members of the radical wing of the Republican party who wanted slavery ended immediately and a hard line policy toward the South. Salmon Chase of Ohio, secretary of the treasury, represented the "iron-back" or Radical Republican point of view in Lincoln's Cabinet.

<u>blue and gray</u>. The colors of the respective uniforms during the Civil War. Union troops wore blue, Confederate troops, gray.

<u>Copperheads</u>. A political party dominated by Democrats in the border states and in Ohio, Indiana, and Illinois. Its members opposed all measures in support of the war and wanted to force a negotiated peace.

<u>Alexander Stephens (1812-1883)</u>. Vice President of the Confederacy who often disagreed with the policies of President Jefferson Davis. At one point he even urged his native Georgia to secede from the Confederacy. Stephens served in the House of Representatives from 1843-1859 and again after the war, 1873-1882.

<u>Monitor vs. Merrimack</u>. A naval battle fought near Virginia on March 9, 1862, between the Union's <u>Monitor</u> and the Confederacy's <u>Merrimack</u>. It was the first fight in history between armored warships as opposed to wooden ones, and the <u>Monitor</u> won.

<u>Bureau of Colored Troops</u>. A governmental agency set up in 1863 to supervise the enlistment of Negroes, who had been officially, at least, barred from the army by a law of 1792. The troops were segregated (and remained so until after World War II) and commanded by white officers. They were paid one half the salary of their white counterparts. By 1865 one Union soldier in eight was black.

<u>General Ambrose Burnside (1824-1881)</u>. A Union general who was commander of the Army of the Potomac for a brief period in 1863. He replaced General McClellan and was replaced by General Joseph Hooker after Lee's army defeated his forces at Fredericksburg. Burnside was famous for his side whiskers, a type which have since been called "sideburns."

<u>National Union ticket</u>. A term used by the Republican party to attract votes in the 1864 election. Abraham Lincoln was renominated. The vice presidential candidate was Andrew Johnson of Tennessee, a former Democrat.

GLOSSARY

<u>battle of attrition</u>. A constant wearing down of the resources of the enemy. In 1864-1865 in Virginia General Grant fought a slow and grinding battle of attrition, never giving Lee's army a chance to catch its breath, to increase its numbers, or to resupply.

breastworks. Temporary, quickly constructed fortifications, usually breast-high. At the siege of Petersburg, Virginia, in 1864, both armies constructed complicated lines of breastworks and trenches, running for miles in a great arc.

Celt. A term sometimes used to refer to the Irish. The feeling against the Irish after they participated so vigorously in the 1863 New York draft riots could be seen in an article in the Atlantic Monthly which stated, "It is impossible to name any standard...that will give a vote to the Celt and exclude the negro." Originally the term Celt referred to an ancient tribe which lived in central and western Europe from around 2,000 B.C. to 400 B.C. and spread its culture throughout the area, including the British Isles.

coup de grâce. A French term which literally means a stroke of mercy. It means a finishing or decisive stroke, as to someone who is mortally wounded. After the battle of Shiloh in 1862, the victorious General Grant was still too shaken by General Johnston's unexpected attack and too appalled by the Union's huge losses to apply the coup de grâce that might have ended Confederate resistance in the West.

greenbacks. Paper money issued by the Union during the Civil War which could not be turned in, or redeemed, for an equal amount in coin. It was simply printing press money, not backed by gold in the treasury.

martial law. Temporary rule by military authorities imposed upon a civilian population in time of war. During the Civil War Lincoln did not hesitate to apply martial law to conquered areas.

materiel. The equipment and supplies, such as guns and ammunition, of a military force. Do not confuse the word with material.

Negrophobes. People who dislike Negroes. Many of the participants in the New York draft riots of 1863 were Irish laborers who were Negrophobes.

pontoon bridges. Temporary floating bridges using pontoons for support. A pontoon is a flat-bottomed boat or other portable float. To occupy Fredericksburg, Virginia, General Burnside's divisions crossed the Rappahannock River over pontoon bridges.

Victorian standards. Characteristics of the period of Queen Victoria, ruler of the British Empire from 1837 to 1901. There was particular emphasis on being morally straitlaced, at least on the surface, with a stuffy, almost pompous air. Topics pertaining to sex were taboo in "polite society." Some of Lincoln's metaphors, or figures of speech, were considered slightly risqué, or naughty, according to the Victorian standards of the day.

West Point. A military reservation in New York which was the site of a Revolutionary fort guarding the Hudson River. In 1802 it became the location of the United States Military Academy, a college to train the country's military leaders. During the Civil War generals on both sides had been educated at West Point. Other service academies have since been founded, such as the United States Naval Academy at Annapolis (1845) and the United States Air Force Academy at Colorado Springs (1954).

Zouave. A member of a French infantry unit, originally composed of recruits from the French colony of Algeria in Africa. Zouave was the French adaptation of Zwawa, an Algerian tribal name. The group was known for its brightly colored and exotic-looking uniforms and precision drilling. During the Civil War there were militia companies on both sides which adopted the name, such as the "Louisiana Zouaves."

OFFICERS IN THE MILITARY

Army	Navy
General	Admiral
Lieutenant General	Vice Admiral
Major General	Rear Admiral
Brigadier General	Commodore (wartime only)
Colonel	Captain
Lieutenant Colonel	Commander
Major	Lieutenant Commander
Captain	Lieutenant
First Lieutenant	Lieutenant (junior grade)
Second Lieutenant	Ensign

DEFINE THE FOLLOWING, USING THE DICTIONARY IF NECESSARY

audacious
bipeds
disapprobation
interregnum
logistical
pandemonium
preponderant
sartorial
vise
vitriolic

SAMPLE QUESTIONS

MULTIPLE CHOICE

1. Which was not an advantage possessed by the North over the South at the outset of the Civil War?
   a. a superior transportation system.
   b. larger navy and merchant marine.
   c. superior military leadership.

d. diversified industrial development.

2. The South hoped for England's aid in the Civil War chiefly because of England's:
   a. defense of slavery in her own colonies.
   b. resentment against the United States government's action in the Oregon question.
   c. sympathy with the South on grounds of religion.
   d. need for cotton.

3. During the Civil War Negroes were:
   a. integrated into Union troops.
   b. only allowed to serve as paramedics.
   c. segregated into their own units.
   d. were not allowed to fight.

4. Which of the following abolished slavery in the states of Delaware and Kentucky?
   a. Missouri Compromise.
   b. Emancipation Proclamation.
   c. Thirteenth Amendment.
   d. Wilmot Proviso.

5. Numerous state colleges were founded as a result of land given to the states under the:
   a. Homestead Act.
   b. Morrill Land Grant Act.
   c. National Banking Act.
   d. Pacific Railway Act.

Answer the following by placing a check under Union or Confederacy.

A. Check the side which won the following battles:

	UNION	CONFEDERACY
1. Fort Sumter	___	___
2. Bull Run	___	___
3. Monitor vs. Merrimack	___	___
4. Gettysburg	___	___
5. Vicksburg	___	___

B. Check the side which the following individuals supported:

	UNION	CONFEDERACY
1. Stonewall Jackson	___	___
2. George McClellan	___	___
3. Alexander Stephens	___	___
4. William Sherman	___	___
5. Samuel Chase	___	___
6. Ambrose Burnside	___	___
7. Joseph Johnston	___	___
8. Thaddeus Stevens	___	___

	UNION	CONFEDERACY
9. Jefferson Davis	___	___
10. William Seward	___	___

ANSWERS

MULTIPLE CHOICE: c,d,c,c,b. (A) Union Victories: 3,4,5.
(B) Union Leaders: 2,4,5,6,
8, 10.

16

Reconstruction and the South

CHAPTER CHECKLIST

Reconstruction. The post-Civil War period, from approximately 1865 to 1877, during which the United States confronted the problems of readmitting the southern states to the Union and integrating the freed slaves into society.

READMISSION OF THE STATES

Controversies. Should the southern states be readmitted automatically or should conditions be placed on their admission? If conditions were set, who should determine them, the President or Congress?

1863, Lincoln's ten per cent plan. A program for reconstruction designed by Lincoln and based on his Presidential pardoning power. All southerners, with the exception of high Confederate officials and a few other groups, could reinstate themselves as United States citizens by taking a loyalty oath. When a number equal to ten per cent of those voting in the 1860 election in a particular state had taken the oath, then that state could set up a state government. The only requirements placed on the new governments were that they be republican, that is, representative; they must recognize the free status of all blacks; and provide for Negro education. State governments in Tennessee, Louisiana, and Arkansas were set up under the ten per cent plan, which was heartedly disliked by the Radical Republicans in Congress.

1864, Wade-Davis Bill. Passed by both houses of Congress, this bill would have made readmission difficult. It was disposed of by Lincoln with a pocket veto. It required that a majority rather than ten per cent of the voters take a loyalty oath to the Union. Those who had been officials in the Confederate government or had voluntarily fought against the United States were barred from voting in the election or serving in the subsequent state constitutional convention. The requirements for the new constitutions were that they prohibit slavery and repudiate all Confederate debts. This unsuccessful bill was favored by the Radical Republicans.

1867, Reconstruction Act. The southern states, excluding Tennessee, were divided into five military districts, each controlled by a major general with almost dictatorial power. In order to end military rule and be readmitted to the Union, the states were to call conventions and draw up new constitutions which would give Negroes the vote and prevent former Confederate leaders from voting. If Congress approved the new constitution, and the state legislature ratified the Fourteenth Amendment, then the state would be admitted. The southerners got around this act by not calling constitutional conventions. So Congress passed another Reconstruction Act requiring the military authorities who were occupying the states to register voters and supervise the election of delegates to constitutional conventions. Southerners defeated the new constitutions by not going to the polls, because the law stated that a majority of registered voters had to ratify the document.

1868, Reconstruction Act. A law stating that constitutions were to be ratified by a majority of the voters, not a majority of those who had registered to vote. Finally Congress got its way and the rest of the southern states were admitted by 1870.

ANDREW JOHNSON (1808-1875), 17th President

- --Born in North Carolina and moved to Tennessee where he entered politics as a Jacksonian Démocrat.
- --Member of the state legislature and of the House of Representatives.
- --Governor of Tennessee (1853-1857).
- --United States Senator (1857-1862).
- --As a southerner loyal to the Union, he was appointed governor of federally occupied Tennessee in 1862.
- --Vice President under Lincoln (March 4 - April 15, 1865).
- --President (1865-1869).
- --Impeached by the House and came within one vote of conviction by the Senate in 1868.
- --Elected to the Senate in 1874 and died the next year.

RADICAL REPUBLICANS AND THEIR PROGRAM

Charles Sumner (1811-1874). Leader of the ultra-Radical Republicans who insisted on immediate racial equality. He, along with Thaddeus Stevens, believed that the southerners had committed "state suicide" and should be treated during Reconstruction as conquered provinces. Sumner was senator from Massachusetts from 1851 to 1874, although he was absent for three years while recovering from the caning by Representative Preston Brooks in 1856.

Thaddeus Stevens (1792-1868). A Radical Republican who supported Reconstruction policies which would protect the freedmen and punish the Confederates, although he was willing to compromise to get the votes of less radical Republicans. Stevens represented Pennsylvania in the House as a Whig from 1848 to 1852 and as a Republican from 1859 to 1868.

Benjamin Wade (1800-1878). Senator from Ohio who was a leader of the Radical Republicans. During the Civil War he was chairman of the Joint Committee on the Conduct of the War.

1865-1866, Black Codes. Laws passed in southern states to regulate the legal and employment status of the freed Negroes. The codes varied from state to state and although some represented a considerable improvement over slavery, others were designed to get around the Thirteenth Amendment and placed limitations on their freedom. Some codes recognized marriages and permitted Negroes to sue and testify in court and to own certain types of property. But some states also passed codes stating that freed persons could not carry weapons, take jobs other than farming and domestic work, or leave their jobs without losing back pay.

1865-1872, Freedmen's Bureau. A branch of the War Department designed to coordinate efforts to help the freed slaves. Its most important function was helping them in the job market, defending their right to select their own employer and to receive a just wage. Also the bureau founded schools and provided food and medical care.

1866, Civil Rights Act. A law which declared that Negroes were citizens of the United States; the measure overturned the Dred Scott decision (1857) and was later confirmed by the Fourteenth Amendment (1868). The act also tried to negate some of the Black Codes by declaring that states could not restrict the Negroes' rights to testify in court and to hold property. President Johnson vetoed the bill, feeling that it violated states'-rights, but Congress overrode his veto with a two-thirds majority in each House. The 1866 Civil Rights Act was the first major piece of legislation to become law over the veto of a President. Radical Republicans were afraid that it would be declared unconstitutional so they initiated the Fourteenth Amendment.

1868, Fourteenth Amendment. An amendment passed by Congress in 1866 and ratified by three-fourths of the states in 1868 after southern states had been instructed in the Reconstruction Act that they would not be readmitted to the Union until they did so. The amendment provided that: 1) all persons born or naturalized in the United States were citizens; 2) no state could "deprive any person of life, liberty, and property, without due process of law;" 3) southern states must grant Negroes the vote or have their representation in Congress reduced; 4) former state or national officials who had joined the Confederacy could not hold another office unless specifically pardoned by a two-thirds vote of Congress; and 5) the Confederate war debt was not to be paid. The Fourteenth Amendment was an important milestone in centralizing political power at the national level, for it reduced the power of all the states.

1867, Tenure of Office Act. This prohibited the President from removing officials who had been appointed with the consent of the Senate without first getting the Senate's approval to dismiss them. President Johnson felt this act was unconstitutional and deliberately violated it by dismissing Secretary of War Edwin Stanton, who was in open sympathy with the Radical Republicans. This action gave the Radicals the excuse they had been looking for to impeach Johnson.

1868, Impeachment of Johnson. The President can only be removed from office after being impeached and convicted of "Treason, Bribery, or other high Crimes and Misdemeanors." Impeachment is accomplished by a majority vote in the House of Representatives and conviction requires a two-thirds vote in the Senate, where the case is tried, presided over by the Chief Justice. Johnson was impeached, that is, charged, on eleven counts, most of them dealing with violation of the Tenure of Office Act. This largely political effort on the part of the Radical Republicans to get rid of Johnson was unsuccessful - barely. The Radicals failed by one vote to rally the two-thirds necessary for conviction.

1870, Fifteenth Amendment. A constitutional change which guaranteed the vote to freed male slaves. It stated that the vote could not be denied "on account of race, color, or previous condition of servitude."

POLITICS AND THE ECONOMY IN THE SOUTH

Politics.

Black Republican governments. Governments in the southern states during Reconstruction in which blacks for the first time participated in politics, generally voting Republican. Although Negroes were elected to a number of political positions, the real rulers of the "black Republican governments" were white carpetbaggers and scalawags.

Carpetbaggers. Northerners who came South during Reconstruction and often took advantage of the Negro vote. They were a varied group: idealists eager to help the freedmen, employees of the federal government, and enterprising adventurers. Carpetbaggers got their name from the fact that they often arrived with their possessions in a carpetbag, an old-fashioned suitcase made out of material which looked like a carpet or rug.

Scalawags. White Republican southerners who during Reconstruction cooperated with the Negro either out of a desire to help him or to exploit his vote. Some were planters and merchants who had been Whigs, but most were people from areas that had had small slave populations and who had continued to support the Union during the war.

Union League of America. A club used by white southern Republicans to control the Negro vote. The organization employed secret rituals and symbols to appeal to the Negro and get him to join. Then he had to swear to support the League list of candidates on election day.

Ku Klux Klan. An organization of white southerners which attempted to counteract the activities of the Union League and drive the Negro out of politics. The name is based on the Greek word "kuklos" which means circle. The Klan was strongest from 1868 to 1872 and was a major force in destroying the Radical Republican governments in the South. The Ku Klux Klan which is in existence today is descended from a group which reorganized in 1915. The revived Klan is not only anti-black but also anti-Roman Catholic and anti-Jew.

1870-1871, Force Acts. Laws passed by Congress to protect Negro voters from the Klan. The acts placed elections under federal rather than local jurisdiction and imposed fines and prison sentences on persons convicted of interfering with a citizen's voting.

Economy.

Sharecropping. A system of cultivating the large plantations at a time when there was little cash to pay wages and the freedmen had no money to invest in land or tools. The plantation owner divided up his land into small units, placing a Negro tenant on each one. In exchange for housing, tools, and other supplies, the Negro family provided labor. As rent, the sharecropper agreed to turn over a portion, or share, of his crop, usually 50 per cent.

Crop-lien system. A method of financing agriculture when money was in short supply. Local merchants extended credit to planters for supplies in return for a lien, or mortgage, on the growing crop. At harvest time the farmer turned over his crop to the merchant who marketed it and returned what was left over after paying off the debt. Generally, the local storekeeper or banker would insist that a cash crop, such as cotton, tobacco, or sugar, be planted, thus contributing to a one-crop dependency rather than diversified farming.

ULYSSES SIMPSON GRANT (1822-1885), 18th President

--Born in Ohio and graduated from West Point.
--Served in the Mexican War.
--Resigned from the army and shifted from job to job between 1854 and 1861.
--Became the outstanding Union general in the Civil War and brought the war to conclusion at Appomatox.
--President (1869-1877).
--Believed that Congress should take the lead in running the government, which contributed to a weak presidency.
--Was personally honest, but his administration was racked with scandals.

ELECTIONS

Election of 1872.

Republican: Ulysses Grant
Liberal Republican: Horace Greeley
Democratic: Horace Greeley
--Grant, the incumbent, received the Republican nomination. But a faction of the party, distressed by rumors of corruption and disappointed by Grant's failure to achieve civil service reform, set up their own party, the Liberal Republican. Their candidate was Horace Greeley, eccentric editor of the New York Tribune. The Democrats also nominated Greeley, but Grant carried the election.

Election of 1876.

Republican: Rutherford Hayes
Democratic: Samuel Tilden
--In this election the electoral votes of three states; Florida, South Carolina, and Louisiana were in dispute with both the Republicans and the Democrats claiming a majority in each of those states. Recall that the winner in each state receives all that state's electoral votes. To decide who had won, a special Electoral Commission was established, not to be confused with the Electoral College, which was to decide whether the Republican electoral votes or the Democratic electoral votes would be accepted from those states. The Commission was made up of 5 Representatives, 5 Senators, and 5 Justices, with 8 of them being Republicans and 7, Democrats. A vote of 8 to 7 decided that the Republicans had carried those states, and Hayes was elected president with an electoral vote of 185 to 184 for Tilden. The election is significant because it was settled by compromises rather than a return to the battlefield.

Compromise of 1877. An informal agreement reached between Democrats and Republicans in which the Democrats consented not to contest the election if they were granted certain concessions. Hayes agreed to withdraw the last federal troops from the South, to appoint a southern ex-Whig to the Cabinet, and to push federal funding of internal improvement projects in the South. Thus a Republican became president, but with the troops gone, the South regained control of its political affairs, became solidly Democratic, and the Negro increasingly lost the rights he had gained.

OTHER TERMS TO IDENTIFY

John Wilkes Booth (1838-1865). An actor who shot President Lincoln in Ford's Theatre in Washington, D.C., on April 14, 1865. He and his co-conspirators felt they were avenging the South, not realizing that their hopes for a moderate peace lay in Lincoln. Booth was shot and killed two weeks later when forces surrounded and burned the barn where he was hiding at Bowling Green, Virginia.

Andersonville. The largest Confederate prisoner of war camp for Union soldiers, constructed in Georgia in 1864. In the summer of 1864 it contained 32,000 prisoners, and overcrowding and lack of medical facilities led to the spread of diseases from which almost one-half died. After the war the prison's Confederate commander, Captain Henry Wirz, was charged with murder, convicted, and hanged.

"forty acres and a mule". A slogan widely popular among southern Negroes in 1865. The idea was supported by Congressman Thaddeus Stevens who wanted to confiscate the property of leading Confederates and distribute it among the Negroes. In reality, little land went into the hands of freedmen, who did not have the money to buy tools nor seeds to plant.

Whiskey Ring. A scandal during the Grant administration involving Grant's private secretary, Orville E. Babcock, who was in collusion with Treasury officials to help a group of St. Louis distillers avoid paying taxes on distilled whiskey. The fraud was eventually revealed and 283 persons were indicted although most, including Babcock, escaped conviction.

Wormley Conference. A meeting between Republican and Democratic leaders on February 26, 1877, at the Wormley Hotel in Washington, D.C. This conference was one of a series which led to Rutherford Hayes receiving the disputed electoral votes in exchange for certain concessions to the South.

GLOSSARY

ante-bellum. The term literally means "before the war." In the United States, it generally is used in reference to the pre-Civil War period.

façade. The face or front of a building, or the portrayal of a fake or artificial front or image. When the Electoral Commission met to determine who should receive the votes in the 1876 election, the atmosphere of judicial inquiry and deliberation was a façade. The decision was really made along party lines.

Fort Monroe. A military fort in Virginia where Jefferson Davis was held prisoner from 1865 to 1867. He was then released and never brought to trial for treason.

franchise. A privilege or right granted to a person or group by the government, particularly the right to vote. Negro males were given the franchise by the Fifteenth Amendment. In recent years the term often refers to authorization by a manufacturer to a dealer to sell his products.

levee. An embankment raised to prevent a river from overflowing. During Reconstruction in the South, tax rates zoomed but some of the proceeds were used to rebuild crumbling levees. The same word can also be used to refer to a very formal reception, such as President George Washington's inaugural levee in 1789.

maverick. An unbranded or orphaned calf or colt on the range. The term originated with Samuel Maverick (1803-1870), a Texas cattleman who did not brand his cows. The word also refers to someone, particularly in politics, who does not follow the group. Andrew Johnson was considered a maverick.

Thomas Nast (1840-1902). A political cartoonist who was best known for his cartoons on the Civil War era and also on the corrupt Tweed Ring of New York City. It was Nast who created the donkey and the elephant as the political symbols of the Democratic and the Republican parties.

point of order. In parliamentary procedure it is a question as to whether that which is being discussed is in order or allowed by the rules. If an individual wishes to raise such a question, he says, "I rise to a point of order." Such parliamentary procedures were not always adequately understood by elected freedmen who used them in the Black Republican governments.

Saint Sebastian. A young Roman martyr of the 3rd century who was tied to a stake and killed with arrows for having embraced Christianity. According to the New York Times in 1877, Justice Joseph Bradley was criticized so vehemently by the Democrats for having sided with Hayes rather than Tilden when the Electoral Commission's vote was counted, that he seemed like "a middle-aged Saint Sebastian stuck full of Democratic darts."

Solomon. King of Israel in the 10th century B.C., who was particularly noted for his wisdom. Even a Solomon would have been hard pressed to judge rightly as to whether the Republicans or the Democrats had really won in 1876 in Florida, South Carolina, and Louisiana.

tippling shop. A bar or saloon which sells alcoholic beverages. Under the Black Codes of Mississippi, a person could be arrested as a vagrant if he frequented tippling shops.

Tweed Ring. The corrupt political machine in New York City from around 1859 to 1871 which was notorious for its payoffs and kickbacks. William Marcy "Boss" Tweed (1823-1878) was the political boss and was finally jailed for his activities.

"unredeemed" southern states. The states which were still occupied by Union forces and thus had not reconstituted their own state governments.

DEFINE THE FOLLOWING, USING THE DICTIONARY IF NECESSARY

chicanery
defalcations
diatribes
excoriating
irascible
obloquy
pathological
progeny
recalcitrance
voracious

SAMPLE QUESTIONS

MULTIPLE CHOICE

1. Typical of the Northern approach to the problems of the Negro during Reconstruction:
   a. Black Codes.
   b. Proclamation of Amnesty.
   c. Freedman's Bureau.
   d. Ku Klux Klan.

2. Radical Republicans favored:
   a. the retention of President Johnson.
   b. severe treatment of carpetbaggers.
   c. harsh enforcement of "Black Codes."
   d. Negro suffrage.

3. The Radical Reconstruction Act of 1867:
   a. abolished the Ku Klux Klan.
   b. provided for military control of the South.
   c. left intact existing Southern governments.
   d. was favored by President Johnson.

4. The Fourteenth Amendment did all except:
   a. give citizenship to the freedmen.
   b. cancel Confederate war debts.
   c. free the slaves.
   d. guarantee payment of the Union war debt.

5. The Union League of America:
   a. kept the Negroes from voting.
   b. worked to make the Negroes loyal to the Republican party.
   c. provided food and clothing to the destitute in the South.
   d. elected Lincoln and Johnson in 1864.

Fill in the blanks with the correct term:

1.________________ Term used for Northerners who came to the South during Reconstruction either to help the freedmen or to take advantage of them, and who often tried to manipulate the Negro vote.

2.________________ Term used for white Southerners during Reconstruction, many of whom had remained loyal to the Union during the war, who cooperated with the "Black Republican" governments.

3.________________ The most famous of the secret organizations formed by white Southerners to intimidate the freedmen and to discourage them from participating in politics.

4.________________ By this law the Radical Republicans planned to limit the power of the President by requiring him to seek the consent of the Senate before he removed officials whose original appointments had required Senate confirmation.

5.________________ The Democratic candidate who would have won the election of 1876 if the Electoral Commission had not awarded all the disputed electoral votes to Hayes.

ANSWERS
<u>MULTIPLE CHOICE</u>: c,d,b,c,b.
Fill in the blanks: 1. carpetbaggers, 2. scalawags,
3. Ku Klux Klan, 4. Tenure of Office Act,
5. Samuel Tilden.

77 9 8 7